The Savvy Paddler

A Guide to the Essentials of Recreational Kayaking

By Jim Stamm

• First Edition •

A grateful "thank you!" to all who contributed to make this book possible, helped edit and improve the book, and supported and encouraged me throughout this project.

The Savvy Paddler

A Guide to the Essentials of Recreational Kayaking

First Edition (v1.0, n10)

This book and cover photos © copyright 2018 by Jim Stamm. All rights reserved.

ISBN-13: 978-1973702504
ISBN-10: 1973702509

Photos/drawings used:
- front cover — "Cabin on Arbutus Lake" (color)
- title page — "Cabin on Arbutus Lake" (B & W)
- page 19 — Drawing A — Kayak Hull Shapes
- page 22 — Drawing B — Kayak Rocker
- page 41 — Photo 1 — Kayak Thigh Braces
- page 55 — Photo 2 — Symmetrical vs. Asymmetrical Blades
- page 125 — Drawing C — Aerial view of a river bend
- page 126 — Drawing D — Cross-sectional view of a river bend
- page 214 — "Leisurely Ladies Cruising the Crystal River" (B & W)
- back cover — "Leisurely Ladies Cruising the Crystal River" (color)

About the author — *Jim Stamm has a B.S. in physics, a minor in mathematics, and worked at Motorola for 15 years as a quartz crystal design and software engineer. His love for the outdoors brought him to northwestern lower Michigan where in 1996 he started his own computer consulting and Web site design company.*

Jim has been paddling in one form or another since 1968, beginning with sit-on-top paddle boards (the predecessor to today's stand-up paddle boards) custom-made by his father, well over a decade of canoeing, and several decades of kayaking. He has paddled rivers from very wide to very narrow and from very calm to Class II. His experience includes scores of inland lakes both large and small as well as "big water" paddling on Lake Michigan.

Disclaimer: The author disclaims responsibility for any liability, loss, risk, or injury, personal or otherwise, as a result of the direct or indirect use or application of any of the contents of this book.

Note: This Web page — **www.atic.biz/tsp.html** — provides details about where this book can be found — locally (near the author), on Amazon, and via book distributors.

TABLE OF CONTENTS — QUICK OVERVIEW

I. INTRODUCTION 8
II. RECREATIONAL KAYAKING 11
III. EQUIPMENT AND GEAR 12
    KAYAK 12
    PADDLE 51
    CHOOSING EQUIPMENT — A Quick Summary 61
    SPRAY SKIRT 62
    LIFE JACKET / PFD 65
    CLOTHING 68
    OTHER GEAR 73
IV. RULES AND GENERAL RECOMMENDATIONS 77
    CARDINAL KAYAKING RULES. 77
    GENERAL KAYAKING RECOMMENDATIONS 79
V. PADDLING 89
    EXPLORING THE BASICS 89
    TESTING YOUR KAYAK 99
    PREPARING BEFORE A TRIP 106
    WARMING UP BEFORE A TRIP 106
    PADDLING LAKES (Or Similar Water) 107
    PERFORMING A WET EXIT 115
    PERFORMING AN OPEN-WATER RESCUE 116
    PADDLING RIVERS 119
VI. EVERYTHING ELSE 161
    SHUTTLING VEHICLES 161
    CARRYING YOUR KAYAK 166
    TRANSPORTING YOUR KAYAK 167
    MAINTAINING YOUR KAYAK AND GEAR 175
    STORING YOUR KAYAK 177
    TAKE A PADDLING CLASS 178
    JOIN A PADDLING CLUB 178
    A FEW FINAL THOUGHTS 179
VII. GLOSSARY 180

TABLE OF CONTENTS — COMPLETE

I. INTRODUCTION 8
II. RECREATIONAL KAYAKING 11
III. EQUIPMENT AND GEAR 12
KAYAK 12

- Test Before You Buy 12
- Kayak Characteristics and Features 13
  - Kayak Length 13
  - Kayak Hull Shape 18
  - Kayak Width 21
  - Kayak Keel: Rocker and Rise 22
  - Kayak Freeboard 24
  - Kayak Type: Sit-inside or Sit-on-top? 24
  - Kayak Floatation 29
  - Kayak Bulkheads 30
  - Kayak Bow and Stern Floats 32
  - Kayak Material 35
  - Kayak Weight 37
  - Kayak Cockpit Size 38
  - Kayak Thigh Braces 40
  - Kayak Foot Rests 42
  - Kayak Seat 43
  - Kayak Hatches 44
  - Kayak Rudder / Skeg 45
  - Kayak Deck / Top-side Rigging 46
  - Kayak Paddle Holder 47
  - Kayak Hip Pads 47
  - Kayak Quality 48
- Buying a Used Kayak 48

PADDLE 51

- Paddle Parts 52
- Paddle Length 52
- Paddle Blade Shape and Size 54
- Paddle Blade Angle: Feathered or Unfeathered? ... 55
- Paddle Weight 56
- Paddle Shaft and Blade Material 57
- Paddle Hand Placement 58

TABLE OF CONTENTS — COMPLETE (continued)

- Paddle Type: One-piece or Two-piece? 58
- Paddle Drip-rings 59
- Paddle Hand Grip: Elliptical or Circular? 60
- Paddle Shaft Diameter 60

CHOOSING EQUIPMENT — A Quick Summary 61
SPRAY SKIRT 62
LIFE JACKET / PFD 65
CLOTHING 68

- Clothing Basics 68
- Dry Clothes 69
- Jacket 69
- Rain Gear 69
- Hat 69
- Sunglasses 70
- Glasses 70
- Footwear 70
- Gloves 72

OTHER GEAR 73

- Gear Each Person Should Bring 74
- Gear Each Person Should Consider Bringing .. 74
- Gear Group Leaders Should Consider Bringing .. 75
- Stowing Gear 76

IV. RULES AND GENERAL RECOMMENDATIONS 77
CARDINAL KAYAKING RULES 77
GENERAL KAYAKING RECOMMENDATIONS 79

V. PADDLING 89
EXPLORING THE BASICS 89

- Before Launching 89
- Tips for Launching and Landing 90
- Basic Strokes and Maneuvers 92

    — Going Forward 92
    — Stopping 94
    — Backing Up 94
    — Turning 95
    — Steering 97

TABLE OF CONTENTS – COMPLETE (continued)

— Stability 97
- More Strokes and Tips 98
- Practice Sessions 98

TESTING YOUR KAYAK 99
- Basic Tests 99
- Lean Tests 99
- Taking on Water Tests 100
- Wet Exit Test 100
- Test Your "New" Paddle 103
- Other Tests 103
- Play Around / Experiment 103

PREPARING BEFORE A TRIP 106
WARMING UP BEFORE A TRIP 106
PADDLING LAKES (Or Similar Water) 107
- Recommendations Before a Lake Trip 107
- Recommendations for Paddling Lakes 109
- Recommendations Regarding Winds 110
- Recommendations Regarding Waves 112
- The Biggest Danger 113
- A Final Note 114

PERFORMING A WET EXIT 115
PERFORMING AN OPEN-WATER RESCUE 116
PADDLING RIVERS 119
- River Dynamics 120
  — Moving Across the Current 120
  — The Main Current 121
  — Obstacles in the River 122
  — Turns and Bends in the River 124
  — Obstacles in Turns in the River 127
- Boat Scouting 128
- Recommendations Before a River Trip 130
- Recommendations for Paddling Rivers 133
- Recommendations When You Are In Trouble ... 139
- Recommendations When Someone Else Is In Trouble .. 144

TABLE OF CONTENTS – COMPLETE (continued)

- Responsibilities of Each Member of the Group 148
  - For the leaders of a river trip 148
  - For every person on a river trip 150
  - For the point boat at the front 152
  - For the second and third place positions 153
  - For the TWO sweep boats at the rear 154
  - For the whole group 156
- The Take-out Point 158

VI. EVERYTHING ELSE 161
SHUTTLING VEHICLES 161
- General Shuttling Method #1 161
- General Shuttling Method #2 163
- Special Shuttling Case for Two Paddlers 164

CARRYING YOUR KAYAK 166

TRANSPORTING YOUR KAYAK 167
- Choosing Tie-downs 167
- Transporting on Top of a Vehicle 168
  - Using racks 169
  - Loading on racks when alone 170
  - Using a foam rubber block and strap system 172
- Transporting in a Truck Bed 173
- Transporting on a Trailer 173
- Transporting Inside a Vehicle 174

MAINTAINING YOUR KAYAK AND GEAR 175

STORING YOUR KAYAK 177

TAKE A PADDLING CLASS 178

JOIN A PADDLING CLUB 178

A FEW FINAL THOUGHTS 179

VII. GLOSSARY 180

A Place for Your Notes 214

I. INTRODUCTION

The experience of kayaking is unlike any other I've found. Without a motor or expensive craft you are completely in charge of your own easily-managed vessel. You get to experience being on the water without needing to be in it. You can explore places few people ever get to in a very close-up and intimate way.

Before venturing out or making a purchase. I highly recommend taking the time to learn about kayaks and safe paddling, starting with this guide.

This book contains a thorough set of essential details, rules, and recommendations covering all aspects of recreational kayaking and a little beyond. You'll also find many helpful tips and suggestions. It's written for the technically-minded person who enjoys reading and seeks to gain a full understanding of kayak design and safe kayaking. Although it delves a little into open-water and whitewater kayaking the book's main audience is those paddling single-person recreational kayaks on **flatwater**, sheltered bays and lakes, close to shore on very calm larger bodies of water, and rivers from very gentle through **Class II** (see the definition in the Glossary.)

Note that this book is not a step-by-step, how-to-kayak manual — it is not intended to be. Nor does it come filled with glossy photographs. There are other books out there that do those things quite well.

But this book does provide a good deal of instructional detail, complementing and supplementing other guides, filling in much additional detail and providing further very practical tips and recommendations.

There is not much said about the joy of kayaking which is why you are doing it in the first place. This might be to commune with nature, have a good time with friends, get some outdoor exercise, explore the natural world, or all of the above. We do not tell you how to have fun — that's up to you as you partake in this lovely and simple water sport. But we do help you choose the proper equipment and show you how to be safe when paddling on lakes and rivers, making your experience as positive as possible. As you become a more savvy paddler you'll build confidence and dispel fear, both of which add significantly to the fun you will have.

This book is for anyone new to recreational kayaking as well as those who have been paddling for quite some time. While an advanced paddler may know much of this material it's likely this book will "shed some light" in several areas. Although this not a guide to whitewater or sea kayaking some of that basic knowledge applies and is incorporated as needed.

This book is the result of myriad "lessons learned" over several decades of recreational kayaking by myself and many I know, learning from both those more and less advanced than myself. That experience has been on rivers both large and small, from very wide to very narrow, and from very calm to **Class II**. It includes experience on scores of inland lakes as well as "big water" paddling on the open waters of Lake Michigan. This book also comes from my own study of kayaking as well as detailed recommendations shared among family, friends, and other fellow kayakers over the years.

Please note, as with any water sport, there are many inherent dangers that accompany recreational kayaking. In no way does this book claim to cover all of the dangers or provide everything you need to know. It is also no substitute for professional instruction from qualified experts.

Nonetheless, I believe you will find this to be a very helpful guide. It offers the essentials to protect yourself and those with you against the most common issues, providing solid, reliable recommendations, making your whole kayaking experience much safer and more enjoyable.

This book reads somewhat like a technical manual (not unlike a vehicle owner's manual and rules of the road booklet) to cover all that's needed to help you be properly prepared for safe kayaking. That's a necessary "evil" to get out of the way before the fun can begin. Please take all that's said herein as the required rules and recommended guidelines that exist for any activity. Do not let these discourage you from the sheer joy of paddling!

Note 1: Most (but not all) terms in bold can be found in the Glossary at the end of the book. In fact it goes well beyond those, providing an extensive list of common kayaking and paddling terms as well as additional details, tips, and even a few more advanced techniques.

Note 2: If you read this book from cover to cover you will encounter some repetition. That is intentional to reinforce certain recommendations and/or so those reading only specific portions of the book do not miss any vital tips.

II. RECREATIONAL KAYAKING

This book is for the recreational kayaker using a single-person **recreational kayak** on **recreational kayak water**.

Recreational kayaks, which are described in detail in the next section, are typically between 9 and 15 feet in length. They have a minimal learning curve and are designed for ease of use, stability, and general purpose kayaking. Their characteristics are in between very short whitewater kayaks and very long sea kayaks, both of which are used by more advanced paddlers and are not covered in this book. Tandem (two-person) kayaks are also beyond the scope of this book as they require advanced paddling instruction and skills, and like canoes, require close cooperation between their paddlers.

Recreational kayak water includes several different types:

- **flatwater** — very calm water with good protection from the wind with little or no waves, such as a sheltered bay, small sheltered lake, or very slow-moving sheltered river,
- close to shore on very calm larger lakes,
- and relatively easy rivers — from Class A to Class II. (See **classification of rivers** in the Glossary.)

Going beyond recreational kayak water requires advanced skills and instruction, very "solid" rescue techniques, and usually a kayak more specialized for the water being paddled.

This book assumes that any trips taken are during the daytime for no more than a day. Although quite fun, overnight trips and **touring** are a whole other realm of paddling that involves a lot more gear, planning, and skills.

III. EQUIPMENT and GEAR
KAYAK

The most important aspect of recreational kayaking is following the many practices required for safe kayaking. Second in importance is choosing the proper kayak.

Kayaks come in many shapes and sizes — all have their place. Most kayak models are slightly different from each other, so several of them all the same length and width can have fairly different characteristics — handling, stability, turning and tracking ability, and so on.

> **RECOMMENDATION:** Choose the proper kayak for the type of water to be paddled and your skill level.

A kayak is chosen primarily based on the type of water being paddled, the conditions of that water, and your skill level. The water type might be roaring whitewater, narrow and twisty rivers, wide and quiet rivers, calm **flatwater**, or exposed open water — such as larger lakes, a Great Lake, or an ocean.

Because you likely will be doing a few different types of water, any boat you choose will be a compromise — great for a few types of water, just "okay" for some, and lousy for a few others. Any recreational kayak will likely not be good at the ends of the spectrum (whitewater kayaking, sea kayaking, or both). **The kayak you choose should be a good match for the water you do most often, and not impractical on water you do less often.** It should normally not be outside of your skill level, unless you are in the process of advancing your abilities and are practicing in safe water.

Test Before You Buy

> **RECOMMENDATION:** Always try out any kayak before you buy or acquire it.

Because there are so many variables involved when choosing a kayak, study the recommendations provided here to get yourself started. Before you buy any boat, always sit in it for a while at the store. Play with all the adjustments. Check out several kayaks so you can compare. Some will be more comfortable than others.

Next, rent from local shops and liveries, take classes, and/or borrow several kayaks to "test drive" them in the water. There is no substitute for real-life experience. You can never quite predict how a boat will handle by looking at it or being told about it. It will handle slightly different for different people because of their weight, height, distribution of weight, torso, arm, and leg length, etc. Keep notes about what you like and dislike about each model.

If at all possible, never buy a kayak without paddling it first. Choosing a boat that properly fits you and the water you'll typically paddle is one of the most important aspects towards a positive and pleasant kayaking experience.

Kayak Characteristics and Features

> **RECOMMENDATION:** Learn about the different aspects and parts of a kayak so you can make the proper choice for the type of water you paddle the most. Use the recommendations provided here and other reliable sources, then test a lot of boats.

Kayak Length

A general rule for a kayak: the longer it is, the faster and more efficient it is. Specifically, the longer its **waterline length**, the greater its **maximum efficient hull speed** and the better its *efficiency* — which means it accelerates faster and takes less effort to maintain a given speed.

It's no mistake why racing kayakers want the longest boat possible. And sea kayakers too, although they will take a slighter shorter and wider boat to gain a little stability over a racing kayak. All else being the same, the longer a kayak is the better it **tracks** (goes straight) but the harder it is to turn. Longer boats are narrower and have a **hull shape** more conducive to speed than stability — so they are also tippier (less stable). But sea kayakers and especially racers will sacrifice stability to gain better performance. **Sea kayaks** are most appropriate for open water and least for narrow rivers. Compared to recreational kayaks, longer boats such as sea kayaks have a steeper learning curve to know how to handle them well.

On the other hand, shorter kayaks are the opposite — they turn the easiest, which is why whitewater experts use them because they need to "turn on a dime". All else being the same, the shorter a boat is the poorer it tracks, so on calm water it feels "squirrely", tending to deviate from course and requiring constant adjusting to maintain one's desired direction. It is also slower and less efficient. But whitewater kayakers willingly sacrifice speed and tracking ability for the ability to turn with a minimal amount of effort.

Shorter kayaks are not as fun as longer boats on a lake as they take much more effort to keep moving as well as heading straight. However, compared to the very short **whitewater kayaks**, shorter recreational kayaks are wider with a flatter bottom (generally) so they are more stable (the most stable of recreational models). They are the most appropriate for narrow rivers and the least for open water. They have a very easy learning curve, perhaps the easiest of any kayak.

As we'll soon see, recreational kayaks nicely fill the gap in between the shortest and longest kayaks. They are a great multiple-purpose boat for the casual kayaker.

For the purpose of this book we look at kayaks in five general classes based upon length.

1) **Whitewater kayak** — 6' to 8' long — with a lot of **rocker** for whitewater experts who need to turn very quickly and care nothing about tracking, speed, or efficiency. This boat is not suitable for the recreational kayaker.
   - Best abilities: turning, maneuverability
   - Worst abilities: tracking, speed, efficiency
   - Best for: whitewater **Class III** or higher

   (Note that there are some longer, hybrid whitewater/recreational kayaks that cross over into the 9' to 11' range. These will still have substantial rocker and may come with a **skeg**. There are also older-style Olympic slalom kayaks up to 13'2" in length.)

2) **Short recreational kayak** — 9' to 11' long — good for narrow, twisty rivers. It is very stable and turns easily — not as quickly as a whitewater boat, but much easier than a longer kayak. It's also slower and less efficient than its longer siblings and does not track very well so it is not good on lakes. But it's (usually) lighter and less expensive than longer boats.
   - Best abilities: stability, turning
   - Worst abilities: speed, efficiency, tracking
   - Best for: narrow, twisty recreational rivers

3) **Medium-sized recreational kayak** — 12' long — a nice balance and good compromise of several features. Like shorter kayaks it is still quite stable — helpful on both rivers and lakes. It turns well enough in most situations (even better if you lean it a little), yet is more efficient and tracks better. It still performs reasonably well on narrower, twisty rivers. And on lakes it's not as slow as its shorter cousins.
   - Best/worst abilities: It is not great at anything, but nicely "in between" and reasonable for everything: tracking, turning, stability, speed, and efficiency.
   - Best for: any recreational water, from small to large recreational rivers, **flatwater**, and close to shore on calm lakes

4) **Long recreational / short sea kayak** — 13 to 15' long — not good on narrower, twisty rivers as it does not turn easily, but is okay on wider/easier rivers. It is less squirrelly, faster, tracks better, and more efficient than shorter boats. Although very good on lakes, it's tippier than shorter kayaks and has more of a learning curve.
   - Best abilities: tracking, speed, efficiency
   - Worst abilities: turning, stability
   - Best for: close to shore on large calm lakes, flatwater, and medium to large recreational rivers

5) **Full-sized sea kayak** — 16' to 19' long — designed for long trips on open water. It is very efficient, very fast, and tracks very well. It's also quite tippy and requires more learning and skills to handle properly. Turning one of these is not easy, so river-wise it should only be used on wider and easier ones. It is typically heavier (when comparing kayaks made of the same material) and more expensive. This boat is not suitable for the recreational kayaker.
   - Best abilities: tracking, speed, efficiency
   - Worst abilities: turning, stability
   - Best for: the open water of lakes and oceans

For what it's worth, there are several more types of kayaks, such as racing kayaks (very long, narrow, and tippy, but very fast), tandem kayaks (for two people and come in a variety of sizes), surf kayaks (for surfing waves on a very large lake or an ocean), and fishing kayaks (modified sit-on-top recreational kayaks with a lot of extra features for the angler). Except for the fishing kayak, these require advanced paddling instruction and skills. (And just to be complete, there are also inflatable, pedal-able, folding, wooden, skin-on-frame, and multi-piece sectional kayaks in a variety of sizes.)

Groups 1 and 5 are for the "experts" of those types of boats and intended water. Recreational kayakers should look at groups 2, 3, and 4:

- Those paddling primarily narrow, twisty rivers and only occasionally easy, medium-sized rivers and small lakes will want a **short recreational kayak**.

- Those paddling close to shore on large calm lakes, wide easy rivers, and occasionally calm, medium-sized rivers will want a **long recreational kayak**.

- Those who paddle many types of water, from narrower rivers to close to shore on calm lakes will like the "happy medium" of the **12' recreational kayak**. It's a slight compromise at either end, but a nice balance for most **recreational kayak water**.

Look closely at the water nearby to which you have access and that you feel comfortable paddling. If you paddle any kind of water on a regular basis you can expect your skills to improve, so you'll be able to handle more than just the very calmest water after a while. **The type of water you will be paddling and your skill level are the most important factors when choosing a kayak.**

Because of the benefits of a short boat (primarily stability), a lot of beginning kayakers start with a short recreational model. Depending on the type of water that will most often be paddled, that may not be their best choice. Beginners are much better off buying the kayak designed for their intended water and getting used to that right away, than to start with the shortest kayak and later having to move to the proper one for the water being paddled. By doing to they also get to immediately experience the benefits of the longer kayak and not be turned off by the negative aspects inherent with the shorter boat.

A related story...

We started my Mom out (at age 65!) in a basic 9-foot recreational boat to get her used to kayaks. That boat was very stable, and being so short even with a flat keel it was very easy to steer. But we found the kayak was too "squirrelly" for her — on calm water it always wanted to turn left or right and was hard to keep going straight. So we had her try a 12-foot recreational kayak with a similar hull shape. She was much happier with that. Being longer it was faster and more efficient (less effort to go the same distance). It tracked much better so she did not have to spend all her time and effort continually correcting the boat's direction. Yet the kayak was still quite stable. She was a "happy paddler".

Look for a sweet spot...

When paddling very narrow (25' wide) and twisty rivers, such as some of those found in northwestern lower Michigan, I would not recommend a 13-foot (or longer) kayak. To be sure, on lakes it is slightly better than a shorter boat. But on rivers it's just long enough to be noticeably harder to turn on the narrowest stretches and catches more easily on tree-fall and other obstacles one is trying to avoid. Also, an 11-foot kayak is just fine as it turns a little easier than a longer kayak on narrower rivers. However, on more open sections the 11-footer is not as efficient and one has to work harder to keep it going straight and keep up with even a 12-foot boat. (All kayaks have a **maximum efficient hull speed** based on their length — even a one-foot difference can mean a lot.) I've found the 12-foot-long kayak is a good "sweet spot" in between. It offers a nice combination of characteristics that allows it to do lakes and rivers (both large and small) all fairly well.

For the combination of different types of water you'll paddle most often, you too may find a single boat that fits your "sweet spot". Although do not be surprised if more than one kayak is needed to best fit your favorite waterways.

Kayak Hull Shape

The bottom portion of a kayak including the sides is called the **hull** — most of which will be in the water.

After length, the shape of the hull is the next most important aspect to consider. Look at the cross section of the bottom across the width of the boat at its widest point (**beam**). Is the central 80% of the bottom flat, almost flat, shallow V-shaped, deep V-shaped, or tending towards a semi-circle?

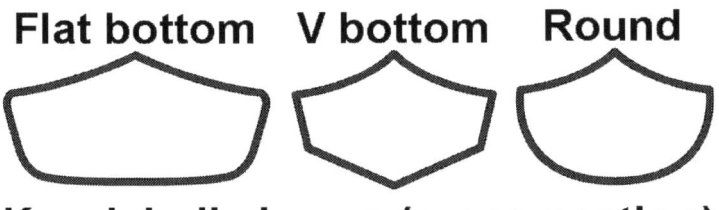

Kayak hull shapes (cross section)

Drawing A — Kayak Hull Shapes

In order, they go FROM: the most stable, yet are the slowest, accelerate the worst, and the least efficient, TO: the least stable ("tippiest"), yet are the fastest, accelerate the best, and the most efficient. (By the way, the most efficient hull with the least amount drag is one with a perfect semi-circular cross section. But good luck trying to stay upright in such a craft. They are like sitting on a floating log — sneeze sideways and you'll find yourself upside down!)

- Whitewater boats usually have a flat or almost flat bottom.
- Recreational boats typically have an almost flat to shallow V-shaped bottom.
- Sea and racing kayaks typically have a deep V-shape or round, almost semi-circular bottom.

Flat or nearly flat bottom hulls are preferred for rivers, because with all else being the same, they turn easier and catches less on the bottom and objects one is passing over.

V-shaped hulls are slightly less desirable for rivers because with their slightly deeper **draft** their bottom catches more easily on a shallow river bottom or logs or rocks one is passing over.

V-shaped hulls are also slightly less desirable than flat bottom hulls as they are a little less stable (but do have decent secondary stability).

Otherwise V-shaped hulls are desirable for their speed, efficiency, and tracking ability.

For what it's worth, some high-end materials allow more complex hull shapes, such as the "gull wing" which is a slightly concave flat bottom but with a narrow, pointed keel running the length of the boat. That shape provides greater stability such as what's needed in a fishing kayak but is something you are not likely to see in common recreational kayaks.

If you want to get fancy also look at the **chine** part of the hull, which is the line of intersection of the bottom with the side of the boat. It might be a "hard" chine — a very sharp edge as seen on the V-bottom hull in **Drawing A**, or a "soft" chine — a rounded edge as seen on the flat-bottom hull in **Drawing A**. Hard chines provide more stability and control for carving a turn while **edging** — a good choice when you want stability in calm water. Soft chines are more efficient, more forgiving, and more predictable when the kayak contacts a shallow river bottom — a good choice for moving water.

Another story...

My Dad built three kayaks from scratch, all the same length and width but experimenting with the hull shape.

The first had a perfectly flat bottom from "stem to stern" and side to side with hard **chines** and abrupt **rises** at each end. This gave the boat the absolute shallowest **draft** and most stability one can expect from a practical hull shape. Because of its low draft, it did not get caught on the river bottom like other similar-sized kayaks. However, it was slow! And with no **rocker** it did not turn very easily. That design is the least efficient and slowest for a practical hull shape. So it was not fun on lakes but was useful on rivers with the help of the current, and was handy for fishing and photography because of it's extreme stability.

The next kayak he built had a shallow V-bottom. This shape had a little more **draft**, but it was much faster (accelerating quicker) and more efficient. He also added a little bit of **rocker**, which along with the hull shape, helped it turn better. But the stability was "uncomfortable" as the boat always seem to lean a little to one side or the other. (An issue not uncommon with V-bottom kayaks.)

With his third kayak he hit a nice compromise. The bottom was almost flat, but not quite, over 80% of the area. But he also added soft **chines**, so it very much resembled the "flat-bottom" hull shape in **Drawing A**. It too had a little bit of rocker, which helped it turn. The draft was in between that of the first two boats. The stability was not quite a good as the first, but still pretty good and it did not have the wobbly feeling of the second kayak. And although not quite as efficient as the V-bottom, it was still significantly better than the perfectly flat bottom boat.

For the same reasons, the flat-bottom hull shape in **Drawing A** is the one that I prefer in a recreational kayak.

Kayak Width

Look at the width of a kayak at its widest point (**beam**). The shape of the hull combined with the width of the kayak affects the boat's stability. Given two boats that have everything the same except the width, the wider boat will be slightly more stable but slower and less efficient. The narrower one will tippier but slightly faster and more efficient.

With **sit-inside kayaks**, full-sized sea kayaks are the narrowest and recreational kayaks the widest. Typical recreational kayaks are between 24" an 34" wide. Shorter sit-insides are generally wider that longer models. **Sit-on-**

tops kayaks are usually a few inches wider than similar length sit-inside boats.

Kayak Keel: Rocker and Rise

Look at the **keel** — the longitudinal center of the bottom of the hull. Set the kayak on a flat surface then lie down next to it looking at it from the side. How much **rocker** is there? That is, how much does the keel curve versus remain flat (parallel the ground) over the central 90% or so of the portion that's below the waterline? Also, look at the **rise** — the keel at the ends going up to meet the **deck** or **top-side** and mostly above the waterline — does it happen gradually over many inches or happen abruptly only near the very end?

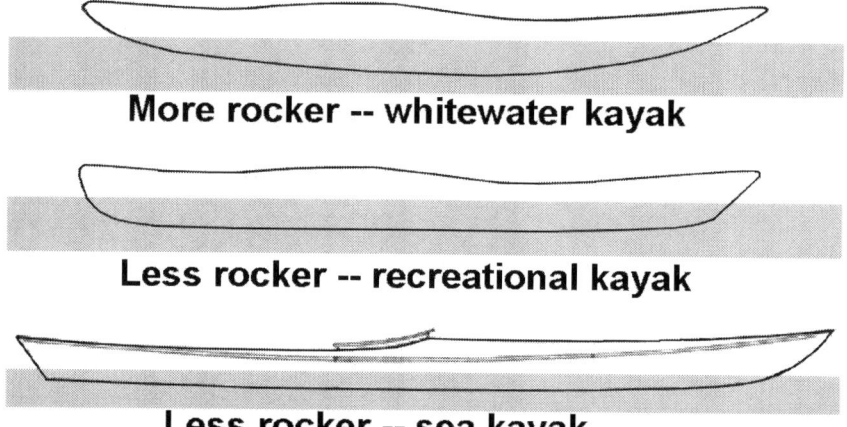

Drawing B — Kayak Rocker

The more rocker and gradual the rise the easier the boat will turn but the poorer it will track. (Think of a saucer that kids ride spinning in the snow.) This is very desired in whitewater kayaks as they need to turn instantly. Just don't expect the boat to track well at all!

On the other hand, the less rocker and the steeper the rise the better the boat will track but the harder it will turn. Imagine a keel with almost no rocker and rather abrupt rises — that is, the keel stays nearly flat until very near the ends. There's a lot more of the hull in the water at the ends of the kayak. It will go straight very well but be difficult to turn. (Think of trying to turn with the long skis of a ski jumper.) This is very desired with sea kayaks.

Keels for recreational kayaks fall somewhere in between the extremes of the whitewater and sea kayak and vary depending on the boat's intended use.

Tip: To turn a kayak with very little rocker, lean it, but not your upper body, as far as you can to one side. You've now just increased the rocker and the boat will turn more easily.

Special case 1: Beware of a kayak with a very abrupt rise in the bow if it will be used in a river that's likely to have obstacles (as most rivers do). Usually you want the ability to go over an obstacle, if you choose, such as a mostly-submerged log, or one that will sink a bit as you go over it. But if the rise is too steep, when you encounter such an obstacle, the bow may catch on it bringing you to an abrupt halt rather than rising over it as desired. You are now in a precarious position that's difficult to get out of unless the current is quite gentle. (I've been in situations where I wished I had a shallower rise in the stern, as well, such as when backing up over an log, but fortunately those cases are rare.)

Special case 2: There are a few kayak models that what might be called a "reverse rise" at the stern. They have a relatively flat keel that extends a few inches PAST the end of the deck or top-side then abruptly angles up and forward from the bottom to connect with the back of the top of the boat. (So the bottom of the boat sticks out past the back of the deck or top-side.) This extends the waterline length of the kayak making it ever so slightly faster and efficient, and track better. But there's a huge problem with this. When you are moving backwards and need to go over a log, branches, through loose pebbles and/or sand — which others and I have needed to do many times — this weird back-end will dig into a soft river bottom and catch on logs and such. It could even bury the back-end of the boat under a log! Therefore, it is recommended that this type of kayak NOT be used for any serious river use.

Kayak Freeboard

A minor consideration for recreational kayakers anyway, is the amount of freeboard — the vertical distance from a boat's **waterline** to the **gunwale**.

Kayaks with more freeboard catch more waves and wind from the side. (Also, with a sit-inside kayak, the more the deck is arched across the width, the more wind is caught from the side.) More freeboard in a sit-inside also provides more storage area and likely more room for your legs. When **edging** or paddling in waves or "bumpy" water, boats with more freeboard will take in less water. But you are more likely to bump your elbows when paddling — depending on the height of the bottom of the seat, the height of your torso, and the length of your arms.

On the other hand, kayaks with less freeboard are helpful because they do not catch as much wind and waves from the side. Sea kayaks usually have a low freeboard and a low deck for this reason. But both of those aspects also allow the possibility of more water entering the cockpit (so a spray skirt is essential) and lessen the storage area and leg room.

Kayak Type: Sit-inside or Sit-on-top?

A major consideration is choosing between a **sit-inside** or **sit-on-top** kayak. Both have their advantages and disadvantages.

A sit-inside kayak has a **deck** (the whole top portion of the boat) and you get into it via a hole in the deck called a **cockpit**. A sit-on-top kayak has no deck — you sit "on top" of it in a molded cavity in the **top-side** for your seat, legs, and feet.

Sit-on-top kayaks:

Sit-on-top kayaks are great if you do not mind getting wet and the air and water temperatures are warm. If those are not the case a sit-inside boat is more desirable.

Sit-on-top kayaks have the advantage in that should you tip over or water come aboard, there's no water to empty out. The hull is a sealed unit — although some come with hatches and covers. When paddling most of the water will splash overboard and much of what remains self-bails via **scupper holes**. A little water may remain, however, such as at the bottom of the seat cavity. So unless conditions are quite calm, expect a wet butt most of the trip. In fact, because you are completely exposed, expect at least some parts of you to be wet the entire trip. It's for that reason that, unless the water is very calm, sit-on-top kayaks are not recommended for longer trips, especially multi-day excursions.

Note that not all sit-on-top kayaks have scupper holes, so be sure to look for that feature. Without them, water will pool in the top-side cavities.

Should you tip over with or fall off of a sit-on-top — you simply flip the boat upright and climb back on. (Be sure you are dressed for getting wet and the temperature of the water!) That's easy to do but only in very shallow water.

These types of kayaks are typically at least as stable as the same-length sit-inside kayak, but they are also a little wider and heavier. They need to be wider to compensate for the fact that the paddler is sitting higher, above the waterline, which raises the center of gravity, thus making the boat less stable. But adding width also adds weight. Know that some narrower sit-on-tops are less stable than similar-length sit-inside kayaks because their seat sits higher.

As there is no cockpit to get into there is much more freedom to move around and some new kayakers feel less intimidated. On the other hand, other paddlers feel more exposed. There is also no support for one's knees allowing them to fall sideways which can become uncomfortable over time.

With no cockpit or knee support one has very little control when needing to lean the kayak or recover from an off-balance situation. One solution is to add **knee straps** as an accessory. These try to pull your knees apart, so when you squeeze your knees together they pull tight, giving you a little bit of control over the balance of the boat. These are better than nothing, but the control is not nearly as good as in a sit-inside boat with decent thigh braces. And the straps are likely to be uncomfortable over time.

Sit-on-top kayaks come with either adjustable foot pedals or a series of notches molded in place to brace one's feet. See the upcoming "Kayak Foot Rests" section for more details.

See the upcoming "Kayak Seat" section regarding seats in both types of kayaks.

No boat is unsinkable, but a sit-on-top kayak is close as the top-side is sealed to the hull. In some models there are accesses to hatches in the interior of the hull, but if the covers to these are open or leak, the boat will begin to fill with water which may not be noticeable at first and can take a good deal of time to drain.

> **NOTE:** Some people choose a sit-on-top kayak for the wrong reason. They think (incorrectly) that they will be "trapped" in a sit-inside kayak if it tips over.
>
> This likely comes from seeing pictures of original Inuit sea kayaks with very small cockpits. For the same design reasons "modern" sea kayaks also have relatively small cockpits compared to recreational kayaks. Those cockpits are designed to be small on purpose as they allow you to hold yourself in place, should you choose to, such as

when **edging** or doing a roll — you don't want to fall out! The impact of any wave or water is also much less with a smaller cockpit. And yet one can still very easily slide out if desired.

However, the cockpits in most recreational kayaks are much larger than in sea kayaks, and some are huge — so large that it would be very difficult to hold yourself in the boat even if you wanted to! In most cases the cockpit in a recreational sit-inside kayak is so large that your knees and perhaps more of you are not fully covered, so when you tip over you will simply fall out. You are not trapped in any way as originally feared.

Therefore, one should not select a sit-on-top kayak merely because it is open on top (no deck) and there is no cockpit to get into.

Sit-inside kayaks:

A sit-inside kayak, on the other hand, has the advantage of being able to keep the part of you that's in the boat (especially under the deck) dry the entire trip. At least some of the water that splashes on to these kayaks runs off the deck. In calm water all of you should stay dry, which is very important if the air and/or water temperature is not warm.

However, should the boat lean over significantly enough to take in water via the cockpit, or if you encounter waves or "bumpy water" that splash into the cockpit, you will get wet and take in some water. A little is okay and manageable; a lot of water is not.

Fortunately, just as whitewater and sea kayakers do, you can use a **spray skirt** — a waterproof fabric that seals around your waist and the cockpit **coaming**. This prevents any water from entering the boat. It has the extra advantage of holding in heat on colder days. If you expect to paddle anything beyond calm water, lean over significantly (on purpose or accidentally), or encounter waves or bumpy water, a spray skirt is highly recommended.

Taking in a little water is not serious, especially if you have bow and stern **bulkheads** or **floats**. Then with a hand-operated **bilge pump**, bailer, scoop, or even a large sponge, you can remove much of the water. But if you take in any significant quantity of water, you will need to get to shore as soon as possible to empty it out. This is even more vital if you have no bulkheads or floats. (It's easy to see why a spray skirt is so important.)

Also, if a sit-inside kayak capsizes it will **swamp** (fill with water). That's a surprisingly heavy amount of water, up to several hundred pounds, especially if there are no bulkheads or bow and stern floats. (Remember, a gallon of water weighs eight pounds.) To recover from this situation one needs to know how to perform an **open-water rescue** and bail out the boat "at sea", or get to an accessible shore as soon as possible to empty it out. (This reinforces why experts out in open water have to wear a **spray skirt** and know how to **roll**.)

Because a sit-inside kayak can hold water and there's a chance it can become swamped, bow and stern **bulkheads**, or at least good **bow and stern floats**, are a must. A **spray skirt** is also highly recommended in anything beyond calm conditions.

Some models of sit-inside kayaks have **thigh braces** which are a huge advantage over a sit-on-top as they allow the paddler way more control when leaning the boat or recovering from an off-balance situation — very important whenever in water that's not perfectly calm. These are covered in the upcoming "Kayak Thigh Braces" section.

As you are in a cockpit in a sit-inside kayak you are also less exposed to the elements but there is less room or freedom to move around. This varies greatly with the size of the kayak and the cockpit. Being in a cockpit can feel intimidating or comforting to new kayakers.

Sit-insides come with adjustable foot pedals — see the upcoming "Kayak Foot Rests" section.

See the upcoming "Kayak Seat" section regarding seats in both types of kayaks.

Kayak Floatation

Sit-on-top kayaks do not need additional floatation because it's built-in due to the sealed or enclosed hull.

Sit-inside kayaks DO require **floatation** of some form. That can be watertight **bulkheads** (the best), **bow and stern floats** (good), or foam rubber **pillars** (just barely adequate). Recreational kayaks often have two different types of floatation such as a bulkhead at the stern and a foam pillar at the bow.

Bulkheads and bow & stern floats are covered in upcoming sections. They provide flotation by preventing water from filling all of the boat and should allow it to float when it's filled with water while you're in it.

If a sit-inside kayak does not have a bulkhead, it should come with a pillar of foam rubber at that end — typically, a vertical piece that's 4" thick held in place in some simple way. If the boat has only these pieces of foam at each end, should it start to take on water, the kayak will still be paddle-able but much harder, and it will be slower and less stable. Water will slosh from side to side and end to end. (Remember that water weighs eight pounds per gallon, so if you've taken on just five gallons of water you have 40 pounds of weight moving about.) If the kayak fills with water with you in it, **it will sink**. But, it should just barely float with you out of the boat. So at a bare minimum make sure these foam rubber pieces are present at each end and securely held in place. (In the whitewater world the foam pillars are very important in the unlikely event the kayak is pinned against an obstacle with the current attempting to collapse it.)

An empty kayak with no floatation will sink and that will happen even before it's filled with water.

Therefore, for a sit-inside kayak that does not have a bow or stern bulkhead it is highly recommended that you install a **bow** or **stern float** of some type.

Kayak Bulkheads

Sit-on-top kayaks do not have or need bulkheads. Sit-inside kayaks require bulkheads or **bow and stern floats** to keep water from filling up the ends of the boat anytime water is taken in.

A bulkhead is a cross-sectional wall inside the kayak's hull that strengthens it and is usually used to seal out water between sections of the boat. (There were bulkheads on the Titanic, but they did not go all the way to the top, so water spilled over from one "section" to the next. The owners or designers carelessly thought full, watertight bulkheads were not needed. Oops!!!)

In a recreational kayak, a bulkhead is typically a single piece of 2" thick, closed-cell (does not hold water) foam glued in place. This creates a relatively dry storage compartment or **hatch**. Access to this is made via an opening in the deck of the boat and covered with a watertight **hatch cover.**

> **Note:** Although the compartment created by the bulkhead is supposed to be a dry storage area, bulkheads and hatch covers can leak and water often finds its way in, especially during a capsize. Always put anything you value in a **dry bag** or **dry box** as well when stowing gear in one of these hatches.

Kayaks can have a bow and a stern (front and rear) bulkhead. The bow bulkhead is just in front of the foot rests and the stern bulkhead is just behind the seat. Some kayaks have an extra one near the cockpit creating an additional hatch, called a **day hatch**, to provide a quick-access compartment to use while paddling.

All sea kayaks have bow and stern bulkheads. Longer recreational kayaks usually have both, as well. Some shorter recreational models have just a stern bulkhead. Cheaper recreational kayaks have no bulkheads, but should have a piece of foam rubber at the ends, usually in the form of a **pillar**. These may be enough to keep just the boat afloat when it's filled with water.

If a kayak has both a bow and a stern bulkhead, **it will float**, but just barely, even with you in it and the entire cockpit area filled with water. The kayak is still paddleable but much harder, and it will be very slow and unstable. But at least you can make it to shore, assuming you stayed close, as any savvy recreational paddler knows to do following **CARDINAL RULE IV**.

If a kayak has only a stern bulkhead, as you'll find in many recreational kayaks, if the boat should fill with water (bow and cockpit areas), it will NOT stay afloat with you in it. It will likely float, however, with you out of the boat. Therefore, make sure you add a **bow float** of some type.

If a kayak has no bulkheads, as you'll find in many inexpensive recreational models, if the boat should fill with water (bow, cockpit, and stern areas), it will NOT stay afloat with you in it or out of it — **it will sink** even before it fills with water. Therefore, it's imperative that you add **both bow and stern floats** of some type. (More about those in the following section).

To summarize — anytime a kayak takes in water the less the better. Therefore bow and stern bulkheads are highly recommended, and if either is missing, add a float at that end.

Tip: If your kayak comes with bulkheads, when you purchase it ask the shop to find out the recommended sealant that will adhere well to both the bulkhead and the hull materials. Then be sure to inspect the bulkheads for water tightness at least once a year — more often if you use the boat a lot — and reseal them if needed.

> **RECOMMENDATION:** If you are buying a sit-inside kayak try to buy one with bow and stern bulkheads. If one (or both) are not present, add a float where the bulkhead is missing.

Kayak Bow and Stern Floats

Sit-on-top kayaks do not have or need floats, they are only needed with sit-inside kayaks where bulkheads are not present.

A float acts similar to a bulkhead and prevents water from filling up the end of the kayak. Should the boat become filled with water, the float helps it to stay afloat while you paddle to shore to empty it out.

If you have not yet purchased a kayak, look at the bulkheads that come with your desired model to determine if bow and stern floats are needed. You'll need to acquire or make floats designed to fit that specific kayak that completely fill up the space at the end and be held securely in place. It's best to determine how this will be handled now before buying anything.

If you already own a kayak that requires floats, shop around to see if **float bags** — inflatable waterproof bags that fit in the bow or stern — specific for your model are available. Make sure they completely fill up the space at the end. Some models of float bags are available that can be opened and resealed and therefore used as storage bags for cargo — very useful when **touring**.

If there are foam **pillars** in place in the bow and/or stern, leave those in place (they keep the kayak from collapsing under certain conditions) and use two smaller float bags to fill the space.

Make your own float:

If you cannot find float bags specific for your kayak, or they do not properly fill the space at the end, you can make your own bow and stern floats. You can use any material that floats to shape and fill the space at the end of the boat. For the bow, this is from just in front of the foot rests forward to the point. For the stern, this is from just behind the seat all the way back to the end. You can shape pieces out of closed-cell (such as **minicell**) foam, or fill the end with floatable material such as bubble wrap or floating packing peanuts — there are many possible choices.

If you use a lot of smaller pieces such floating packing peanuts, follow this procedure:

1. Find a large trash bag (or similar) a little taller than the length of the space to be filled. (It will not hurt to use two bags, one inside the other.)
2. Stand the kayak on the end to be filled.
3. Put a small inside-out loop of duct tape on the bottom end of the bag.
4. With a broom handle (or similar) inside the bag, push the bottom end of the bag into the end of the boat and try to make the tape stick. If it did, remove the broom handle. If not, leave the broom handle in place for now.
5. Pull the bag up and open, being careful to not lift it or pull it out.
6. Fill the bag with your floating material leaving enough room to tie the bag closed. Pack the material in as tightly as you can, but make sure the bag does not rise up.
7. Remove the broom handle if you had left it in place.
8. Close the top of the bag with a few twist ties. (The main reason for tying the bag closed is not to seal out water,

but to hold all the floating material in place. But if water stays out of the bag, so much the better — that will add to the amount of floatation — but it's not super essential the bag be watertight.)

9. With duct tape, secure the bag in place by running tape around the top edge of the bag, overlapping the tape onto the inside of the boat.

> **RECOMMENDATION**: If you add any floats or float bags to a sit-inside kayak be sure to fully test them before going on any trip.

Test your floats:

Whether purchased or home-made, test out any floats to make sure they work as expected as well as experience what it's like when your boat swamps.

Grab a friend and put on your swimsuits. Find a shallow piece of warm, calm water. Paddle your kayak out into a foot or two of water. Lean it over just enough to take in water and let the cockpit fill about half-way. Are your floats working? Paddle around a little bit to see if they are staying in place and not coming loose, floating away.

Next, lean the boat over some more and let it fill with water. If your floats are working as expected and full enough as is required, the kayak should still float even with you in it.

If the floats are not sufficient enough, the boat will begin to sink. (Later add more floatation). If that's the case, get out of the kayak then manually lean it over a bit to allow it to completely fill with water. Does the boat float now? In not, you MUST add more floatation before using it on a trip. If it does float, that's the minimum acceptable level of floatation. But it's best if there's enough floatation so with the kayak filled with water and you in it, the boat still floats.

When done, take the kayak to shore and with your helper empty out the boat.

In the "TESTING YOUR KAYAK" section we talk about what you'll experience as the kayak fills with water, how the boat's handling is affected, and how to empty a swamped kayak.

Kayak Material

For the common types of recreational kayaks covered in this book there are two general choices of material: plastic or composite.

Durability is key for recreational kayaks especially if you do any river paddling. Ideally you want a boat that you can accidentally drop off your roof rack, **scooch** over logs and boulders, or bash into submerged rocks without worry. Cost and weight are important factors as well. It depends on the type of water you intend to do. Those paddling a lot of rivers will likely find that a slightly heavier, less expensive, yet more durable plastic boat is best. Or you may be willing to sacrifice some durability for a lighter-weight composite kayak if cost is not a concern and are likely to only paddle lakes and wide, easy rivers.

Plastic kayaks:

Most **plastic** recreational kayaks are made with **rotomolded polyethylene**. These are heavier than those made with composite materials but are the least expensive, very durable, and can take a lot of abuse. They have several times the impact strength of fiberglass. In plastic kayaks one can bash into just about anything while paddling and be okay. They are used almost exclusively by whitewater paddlers and rental fleets because of their durability. It was the advent of the plastic boat and the **rotomolding** process that transformed the kayak world, opening up kayaking to "the masses".

Unlike composite materials, plastic is more flexible and more forgiving as it will bend when you hit or go over something. But plastic is softer than composites, so you have to avoid sharp objects, such as the edges of large rocks, the tops of metal fence posts, large nails in manmade river structures, or landing directly on the pointed end of a broken branch as I did once, putting a hole in the boat! Also, polyethylene deforms if improperly stored, especially from prolonged exposure to heat or the sun.

Also, one should never drag a plastic kayak (or any kayak) across any rough surface (such as gravel, concrete, or asphalt), but only on soft surfaces (such as sand, grass, soft dirt, or firm mud). Dragging it on a rough surface will scrape up the bottom and begin to wear it away. Dragging a kayak on its tail is a super "no-no" as doing so will quickly wear through the boat's material, which can break through when least expected and leave a hole that's very difficult to repair.

Composite kayaks:

Composite recreational kayaks are made from materials such as fiberglass, Kevlar, or carbon fiber. They are called *composite* because they are composed from a combination of several materials. For example, fiberglass is layers of glass fiber mixed with various resins, then topped with a gel coat on the exterior.

Composite kayaks are more expensive but lighter than the same boat in plastic. The material is also harder and less forgiving, so in a severe bash they are more vulnerable and can even crack. Therefore, whitewater kayaks never use composite material. But composite boats are less susceptible to tears when scraped across sharp objects.

Dragging a composite kayak on any rough surface is still a "no-no" as it will scrape up the bottom and can still wear a hole through the tail. Fortunately, composite material is usually easier to repair than plastic.

Kayaks built with composite material are also stiffer than plastic versions. This is not a concern with recreational models, but important for longer boats, such as sea, touring, and racing kayaks. A stiffer boat is more efficient, as it does not flex as much as it's paddled, so more of the paddler's energy is used to propel the kayak forward. Serious sea kayak paddlers will always choose a boat made from composite (or similar) material.

Other materials:

There are also kayaks made from other high-end, relatively rigid, strong, lightweight material, such as ABS/acrylic blends and polycarbonate. Although not a composite, kayaks made from these materials have very similar characteristics yet are a bit more durable.

In summary:

Perhaps this table will help...

	Weight	Cost	Durability	Stiffness
Plastic:	Heaviest	Cheapest	Excellent	Flexible
Composite:	Lightest	Expensive	Reasonable	Very stiff

In general, rotomolded polyethylene kayaks are best for beginning, recreational, and whitewater paddlers; composite material boats are best for serious sea and touring paddlers. Of course, there are exceptions — there are some plastic boats that could satisfy experienced sea kayakers, and there are some great recreational composite boats. Learn the characteristics of the different materials, and compare these with your needs and the type of water you'll typically paddle — then choose a kayak that best meets all of your requirements.

<u>Kayak Weight</u>

The weight of a kayak is also a factor to consider, both in and out of the water.

If a boat weighs less, obviously, it's going to be easier to carry and get on and off your roof racks. Of course, you should always paddle with another person, and using two people is by far the easiest way to carry and load/unload a kayak. Still, there are times where you may be carrying or loading/unloading the boat by yourself. Make sure you and your system for carrying and loading/unloading accommodates the kayak's weight. That may mean needing a kayak cart to carry it and a trailer to transport it.

The weight also makes some difference in the water. A lighter kayak displaces less water so it does not sit as deep, making it easier to move through the water. The boat will be more responsive to each input from the paddler. This is usually not a concern for recreational kayakers but very important for serious sea, touring, and racing paddlers.

Kayaks can weight between 20 and 80 pounds, the extreme end of that range will be some specialty type of boat. Most single-person, plastic recreational kayaks are between 35 and 60 pounds. Longer, wider, and sit-on-top boats are heavier, whereas shorter, narrower, and sit-insides are lighter. Expect roughly a 10-pound increase in weight for a comparably-equipped, similar-length sit-on-top kayak over a sit-inside. And there's about a 10 pound decrease in weight for a similarly-equipped, same-length, composite kayak compared to a plastic model.

Many folks feel a 50 pound boat is much too heavy to carry by themselves, yet a 35-pounder is reasonable for short distances.

When choosing a kayak, start with the weight the manufacturer claims, but then pick the boat up yourself and compare it to others in the store. And that's when it's empty such as when loading it on a vehicle. When carrying the kayak to the water the total weight can be 5 to 10 pounds more with all your gear. Then add another 3 or 4 pounds for your paddle.

Kayak Cockpit Size

As sit-on-top kayaks do not have a **cockpit** this section applies only to sit-inside kayaks.

Cockpits (or really the opening in the deck) in recreational sit-inside kayaks come in a huge range of sizes, from small ones resembling that of a full-size sea kayak, to very large ones that would allow you, a small child, and/or even the family dog to come along!

Traditional Inuit-style and a few modern sea kayaks have very small cockpits that are merely a small hole that one must slide into, feet first. These help keep the water out, are the easiest to get a **spray skirt** around, and together with **thigh braces** help hold the paddler in place when **edging** or **rolling**.

This is NOT the case for recreational sit-inside kayaks. A cockpit in any recreational model is large enough that you can sit in it first then bring in your legs. (In fact, even most "modern" sea kayaks have a key-hole-shaped cockpit that's large enough that it does not require sliding in feet first.)

The cockpits in most recreational kayaks are much larger than those found in sea kayaks, and some are huge (perhaps 22" wide by 48" long) — so large that, should you tip over, it would be very hard to hold yourself in the boat even if you wanted to! You would simply fall out. You are not trapped at all as those new to kayaking sometimes fear.

The cockpits in some longer recreational kayaks can also be as small as those found in most sea kayaks (as small as 16" wide by 28" long). These will include **thigh braces** — which are very important for maintaining control of the boat or when rolling. Yet these cockpits are still large enough that one can easily exit the boat if desired.

Tip: In cockpits without thigh braces, especially larger ones, your legs will have a little more room to move around. However, your knees may hit the sides of the kayak. If that's uncomfortable or you want better knee support, consider gluing in some **minicell foam** to alleviate the issue.

Choosing a cockpit size:

When choosing a cockpit size, perhaps the most important factor is how easy is it for you to get in and out. Practice doing this before acquiring any kayak.

Next in importance is the type of water you'll be paddling most often.

If you expect to do mostly very calm water, do not need a spray skirt, need a lot of room to get in and out, want to move around a lot while paddling, and perhaps want to carry a child and/or a dog, a large cockpit makes sense.

If you'll be padding on anything but very easy rivers, or on lakes with waves or whitecaps, a large cockpit is much more vulnerable to taking in water and therefore not recommended.

It's also harder to get a **spray skirt** to seal well or stay in place (not collapse) with a large cockpit. If you expect to paddle water requiring the use a spray skirt, look for a boat with a small or medium-sized cockpit.

Small recreational cockpits have less room to lift your legs and knees out while paddling, but it's still possible. Yet in general you'll be drier and find they are the easiest to seal with a spray skirt.

If you paddle anything other than very calm water, a cockpit with decent **thigh braces** is recommended and that usually requires a small cockpit. (See **Photo 1** in the next subsection.)

Kayak Thigh Braces

Sit-on-top kayaks do not have thigh braces, so this section applies only to sit-inside kayaks.

> **RECOMMENDATION:** If you are buying a sit-inside kayak and the type of water you'll be paddling warrants it, try to buy one with thigh braces.

Thigh braces, sometimes called knee braces, knee hooks, or thigh hooks, are parts added to or molded into (the type shown in **Photo 1**) the area of cockpit opening where your thighs or knees contact the edge of that opening. Or they can be simply a well-designed cockpit opening that crosses over your thighs in a comfortable way. Once in the boat you spread your legs slightly to "hook" them under the braces. Together with your feet on **foot rests** you can "lock" your legs in place. This gives you great control of your kayak when leaning, **edging**, or maintaining your balance. Via movement of your hips you control your boat versus it controlling you. (I'm so used to a kayak with comfortable thigh braces I feel a bit vulnerable without them.)

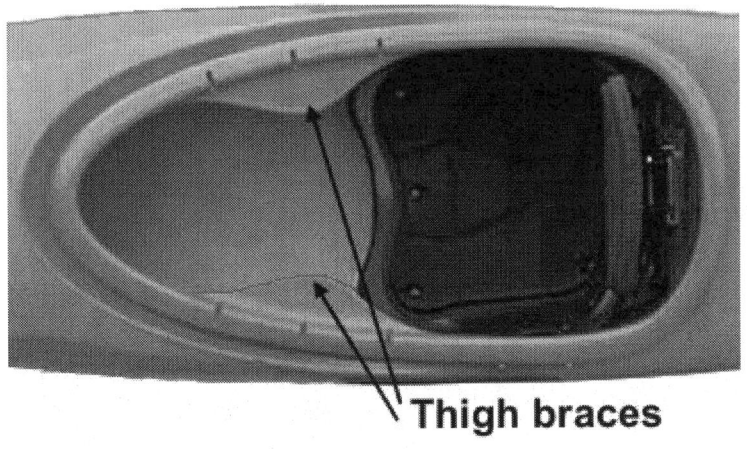

Photo 1 — Fully-fledged Kayak Thigh Braces

Thigh braces are the most important feature for control of the kayak and therefore highly recommended. If you ever expect to be in anything beyond the calmest water, in any situation where you will be leaning (such as when encountering obstacles in a river or turning a longer boat), thrown off balance (such as by wind, waves, current, or obstacles), or holding an edge while paddling, thigh braces (as well as **foot rests**) are essential for maintaining adequate control of the kayak.

A lot of beginning kayakers get a kayak without thigh braces then get freaked out any time the boat rocks from left to right — they feel helpless as they have no control of this rocking and their body gets rocked around as well. Yet, if the kayak has any kind of thigh braces, the paddler can use those to lessen or at least maintain control of this rocking.

Well-designed thigh braces accommodate your knees or thighs well. These can be pieces added to the boat or molded in place. Usually only those kayaks with smaller cockpits have decent thigh braces.

Notice in **Photo 1** that even a small recreational cockpit is large enough that you can sit in it first then bring in your legs. And you can still easily get your knees/legs out of the cockpit when getting out, paddling, or **wet exiting**.

Kayaks with larger cockpits and/or those not so well-designed treat thigh braces as an afterthought, often just adding some padding where your knees touch the edge of the cockpit opening. These are often uncomfortable, hard to get your knees under, and not very effective.

Before you buy a kayak, while on land, adjust the **foot rests**. Then get into it, put your feet on the foot rests, put your knees or thighs under the thigh braces, then press forward on the balls of your feet to "lock" your legs in place. Rock the boat from left to right. Look at how well your knees or thighs fit under the braces and how much control you have of the stability of the kayak.

Kayak Foot Rests

Foot rests are adjustable pedals (in sit-inside and some sit-on-top kayaks) or a series of notches molded into the boat (in some sit-on-top kayaks) upon which you place your feet. Without them, your legs would tend to flop around allowing your body to also flop around. They allow you to hold yourself in the seat and maintain a good posture.

The adjustable-pedal type of foot rests are recommended over the notch type because they offer more choice of position and support the balls of your feet giving you more control. The notch type of foot rests support just a part of your heel.

In sit-inside kayaks, when used along with thigh braces, placing your feet on the foot rests allows you to "lock" your legs in place. This gives you great control of the stability of the boat making it an extension of your lower body — essential in whitewater and sea kayaks and very helpful in recreational kayaks.

Before you buy a boat, make sure it has some form of foot rests. If not, have them added or add them yourself — this is easy to do with sit-inside kayaks.

Kayak Seat

Seats in today's sit-inside kayaks are much more comfortable than they were when kayaks became really popular in the 1990s. They often have padded seat bottoms and the backrests are padded, more secure, and adjustable.

The seats in sit-on-top kayaks can be much less comfortable as they start with a built-in cavity for the seat-bottom, perhaps add some paddling, then have either a hard, non-adjustable backrest, or an adjustable, padded, "floppy" (less secure) backrest that straps to the boat.

It's important to test out the seat of any kayak before you buy it. Learn all of the ways the seat can be adjusted. Make sure it fits you well, is well-padded where needed, and properly supports your back and upper thighs. If the seat normally comes without padding or adjustments, or does not have enough of either of those, ask the store what they can easily add or modify. Consider making your own modifications to ensure you will be comfortable for hours at a time. If you are not, you will not be a "happy paddler" even after a short time in the boat. Determine the following:

- Can the seat be easily adjusted when paddling? This is essential if you are on a trip where there is no easy place to pull ashore.
- Will the seat be comfortable under all the conditions you are likely to paddle and for long periods of time?
- Does it support your thighs and lower back properly?
- Does it allow for good posture?

<u>Kayak Hatches</u>

Some sit-on-top kayaks have watertight storage compartments or **hatches**. Some even make the whole interior of the hull a storage compartment.

Sit-inside kayaks with bulkheads have hatches created by those bulkheads.

Access to any hatch is via some form of **hatch cover**.

CAUTION: An open or even slightly loose hatch cover can be dangerous if you are in any situation where your kayak might take in water in those hatches, even when just leaning the boat!

> **RECOMMENDATION:** Always make sure all hatch covers are on tight each time before entering the water.

These compartments are very handy for all sorts of gear you might want along, from small things such as cell phones, cameras, keys, first aid kit, and a wallet, to large things such as a dry-clothes bag, camping gear, and lunch.

Do not trust any "watertight" hatch to be 100% waterproof! Bulkheads and hatch covers can and do leak, especially in a capsize situation. Hulls can leak. Make sure any gear that can truly not get wet is also stowed in a **dry bag**, and even better, a **dry box**. Put your cell phone, camera, GPS device, radio, wallet, vehicle key fobs, and first aid kits in these. Then stow the bag or box in a hatch.

> **RECOMMENDATION:** Anything that cannot get wet should be put in a **dry bag** or **dry box** and then stowed in a watertight compartment.

Kayak Rudder / Skeg

A **rudder** is a moveable blade mounted at the stern of the kayak. It swivels from left to right, is usually controlled by the foot pedals, and is raised and lowered via lines from the cockpit. When not in use, the rudder rides outside the water, usually on top of the deck.

Although a rudder can be used to turn a kayak its primary function is to help maintain the direction of longer boats when there are strong winds, waves, and/or current — usually on more exposed water. Rudders are not practical and can be in the way on small and medium-sized rivers.

A rudder provides more control and is therefore more effective than a skeg. But with a rudder the foot pedals are not fixed which some paddlers do not like. Rudders also have more moving parts than a skeg so there's more to clean to keep them working properly.

Some kayak models allow rudders to be added later, if desired. Some experts suggest learning to paddle without them first then add them only if absolutely necessary.

A **skeg**, on the other hand, acts like a fixed rudder — it does not swivel but can only be tilted up and down. It's raised and lowered via a line or lever near the cockpit. A skeg usually tucks up into a pocket (called a skeg box) in the stern of the hull so it's out of way when not in use.

The primary function of a skeg is to provide directional stability. It can help with shorter boats that need to track better on calm water and longer boats when they encounter strong winds, waves, or current — usually on more exposed water. A skeg is not needed on small and medium-sized rivers and can be in the way if deployed.

Skegs are advantageous because when not in use they are completely out of the way and cannot catch on anything. And unlike a rudder, with a skeg the foot pedals are not involved and remain fixed.

In a **crosswind** with a skeg fully deployed, the kayak may tend to **leecock** (turn downwind). To accommodate this, a skeg's depth is adjustable — it can be fine-tuned to find the perfect balance so the boat neither **weathercocks** or leecocks but heads in the desired direction.

A "basic" recreational kayak will not come with a skeg or rudder. Consider the water you will be doing most often, the likely condition of that water, the winds on that water, and the boat you'll be using to determine if a skeg or rudder is really needed.

> **RECOMMENDATION:** Determine if you need a skeg or a rudder based on the water and conditions you are most likely to paddle. Note that most recreational kayakers start out without them and never need them. They are not essential.

Kayak Deck / Top-side Rigging

Some sit-inside kayaks have **deck lines** in the form of nylon rope or shock cord. There are two basic types:

1. *cargo lines* going across the deck which can hold items to which you need easy access (such as a jacket, water bottle, sunscreen, spare paddle, or map).
2. *grab lines* along the perimeter of the kayak which help you hold on to it when you're in the water next to it.

Most sit-on-top kayaks have some form of top-side rigging, typically shock cord. Any gear you bring along will need to be secured on board usually via these lines.

With sit-inside kayaks most gear you bring along should be stowed inside the kayak and secured well so it cannot float free in the event of a tip or capsize. But feel free to put a few lightweight things in the cargo lines of the deck rigging, if needed.

Note: Deck and top-side lines should not be used to carry a kayak. They are not designed to support the weight of the boat and may break or their fittings may come loose. Nor should deck lines be used when getting in or out of the kayak. (Instead, run a rope from the bow to the cockpit if needed.)

> **RECOMMENDATION:** Look at the deck or top-side rigging of a kayak you are about to acquire to be sure it's adequate for your needs. If not it may be possible to add your own.

Kayak Paddle Holder

Some kayaks come with a paddle holder, usually a short piece of shock cord and a small hook attached near the cockpit. It can be used to hold your paddle lengthwise on the boat next to the cockpit when it's not in use, such as when fishing or performing a **self-rescue**. It can also hold a fishing rod when it's not in use. A paddle holder is very handy and useful feature and can be easily added if your kayak does not have one.

Kayak Hip Pads

If you do a lot of controlled leaning (**edging**) with your kayak, something you are likely to do as you get better, and find that your hips shift from side to side in the seat, you must not be eating enough carbs! (Kidding, sorry.) If this is happening, this shifting can detract from maintaining proper balance of your boat. Consider installing equal-sized thin pieces of closed-cell (such as **minicell**) foam with waterproof contact cement on both sides of the kayak's seat so that your hips fit snugly in the seat. Take care to not make the fit too tight. This helps make the kayak more of an extension of your lower body giving you even better control overall.

Kayak Quality

Beware of the quality of the kayak brands sold at big box / discount stores and the cheaper brands at sporting goods stores. There's a reason those are so inexpensive — their construction and workmanship is likely questionable. Ideally, purchase a reputable, well-known brand from a dedicated paddle sports store. Before making a purchase, do some research on-line to seek out reviews of the brands and models in which you are most interested. If possible talk to owners of those kayaks, such as at a paddle club, to learn more about them.

Buying a Used Kayak

You may be lucky and find a good, used kayak available for sale. The ones in the best shape tend to get passed down to family members and friends. Nonetheless, sometimes private parties let go of boats that are still in good shape. Local paddle clubs, classified ads, paddle sports stores, and Craig's List are a few good places to look.

Often boat liveries sell older, well-used kayaks from their rental fleets. These are usually not nearly as well taken care of as those owned by private parties and can be significantly scraped up. Be extra vigilant when inspecting these boats. Ask if you can test one for a few minutes in some local water.

Inspect any used kayak very carefully — use your "used-car-buying skills". Here are some of the things to look for:

- Are all the parts present?
- Are all parts that should be, fastened on tight?
- Do all the parts that should move, move easily?
- Look at the condition of all the parts.

- Are there bulkheads? If so, expect to have to reseal them. If not, there should be a foam block, **pillar**, or other type of floatation at each end. If not, you will need to add floats.
- Look at the quality of the workmanship.
- Look for well-known, reputable brands. If it was a Wal-Mart special, don't bother.
- Look closely at any and all seams, if there are any.
- Sit in it and make sure if fits you and your needs well.
- Inspect the hull very carefully, especially watching for any repairs, deep gouges, cuts, cracks, or fractures.
- Look at the bottom to see if the boat's been dragged across rough surfaces, especially at the stern end of the keel where it might be worn thin. (This is especially true with rental boats.)
- Expect the bottom to be scraped up a little, but do not buy the boat if it's scraped up a lot.
- Look for any deformation of the hull or deck.
- Look closely at the condition of any hatch covers and the drain plug, if present. Are they in good shape and do they seal well?
- Look around to see how the kayak was stored and transported, if that's evident. Ask the owner if you feel the need.

Ask the owner:
- Are you the original owner?
- What's the history of the kayak?
- Has it ever been dropped or damaged?
- Has any repair work ever been done on it?
- Is there anything unique or unusual about the boat I should know about?
- Can I test drive it?

If you buy the kayak immediately test drive it looking for any leaks. Besides doing some normal paddling, submerge the whole boat underwater and very carefully watch for any bubbles. With a sit-inside kayak, "seal" the cockpit with a piece clear plastic sheeting and some rope or shock cord pulled tight around the coaming. If you do not do this at least fully submerge one end at a time. If there are any leaks find their source and seal them, then test the boat again for leaks before going on any paddle trip.

PADDLE

Although you are the motor, it's your connection to the paddle and its connection to the water that allows you to do anything in a kayak. You will be using your paddle as many as a thousand times an hour (and maybe more) to control almost all movements of your boat, so it's much more important than you might think at first. (You can, of course, paddle with just your hands. You will have only minimal control over the kayak, but doing so can be fun during a slow float trip on a gentle river on a warm day.)

Just about any double-bladed paddle will work to propel a kayak, from the heavy, wooden, custom-made job by your dad from two old oars (true story), to ultra-light versions used by racers. Both are impractical for the recreational kayaker, however, who needs a paddle that's a nice compromise between weight, durability, efficiency, comfort, and cost.

> **RECOMMENDATION:** Start with a good basic paddle, but move to a better one once you become a little more experienced. Learn all the parts and characteristics of a paddle so that you choose an appropriate one for the type of water you paddle.

There are many aspects of paddles. If you're just getting started, save learning about those for a future paddle you will move up to.

For your first paddle start with one at a reasonable cost that a good kayak store recommends for the type of water you expect you'll paddle most often. Do not go with the cheapest one you can find at Kmart, or a very lightweight one found at a high-end kayak shop. Make sure it will stand up to the abuse you (and your kids?) may give it, in and out of the water.

Know that the wrong paddle for the type of water you're paddling (as well as your skill level and type of kayak) can be very frustrating, whereas the proper paddle will make paddling a much more fulfilling and joyful experience. So that's why, after a little experience, I recommend moving up to a better paddle, one that better fits you, your skill level, and especially the type of water you paddle the most. Take the time to learn about the many aspects of paddles, such as: length, weight, shaft material and diameter, bent shaft or straight, blade material, shape, and size, one-piece or two, feathered or not, fixed or adjustable feathering angle, drip-rings or not, and circular or elliptical hand grip. The following sections will help. Know that a better kayak shop should be able to order a custom paddle to your specification.

Keep your first paddle as a spare.

If you often paddle more than one type of water you may find that you want/need two different paddles, such as one for quick, narrow rivers and another for quiet, open water.

Paddle Parts

All double-bladed paddles have three main parts: the blade at each end and the shaft in between. On each blade are two faces: the **power face** — the front face that catches the water when you paddle forward, and the **back face**. Where the blade tapers to meet the shaft is called the **throat**.

Paddle Length

Watch out for the length. Sometimes stores will sell a paddle that's too long, such as 220 cm (86.6") and as much as 240 cm (94.5")! Whereas for general recreational use I recommend a paddle that's closer 205 cm (80.7") — 6" to 14" shorter than those longer ones. A shorter paddle is lighter than a longer one (made of the same material). It is also more efficient (takes less effort) as the resistance (where it contacts the water) is closer to you so the lever arm is shorter.

Whitewater kayakers use even shorter paddles because they need to make very powerful strokes that require a very aggressive, near-vertical, paddle position.

Sea kayakers, on the other hand, do not need powerful strokes — they make many low-angle relaxed strokes and need to do this all day long. For them it makes sense to have quite a long paddle as they will not be lifting it very high for each stroke. They also do not have rocks and other debris with which a whitewater kayaker has to contend and maneuver around.

If you will only be doing calm, still water (such as very quiet, unexposed lakes) in a sit-inside kayak, a paddle in the 215 (84.6") to 225 cm (88.6") range makes sense. For then, like sea kayakers, you will be making many light, relaxed strokes the whole trip, never lifting the paddle very high with each stroke, and never having the need for more powerful strokes.

Sit-on-top kayaks run a little wider than sit-inside ones, so it makes sense to have a paddle that is a little wider than what would be chosen for sit-inside kayak. Consider a paddle between 220 (86.6") and 230 cm (90.6"). Choose the longer model if you only do calm, still water.

If you are much shorter (or taller) than average, you should likely choose the shorter (or longer) paddle in the range recommended.

For many recreational kayakers it's more likely you'll encounter and be doing a mix of both calm and wavy water, both quiet and moving in a current on a river. And if on a river, no matter how calm, there are always times when a quick, powerful stroke is essential to avoiding a calamity. So again, that's why a paddle that's closer to 205 cm (80.7") is recommended.

No matter what length paddle you have, if you need to reach out farther with it, which is handy once in a while, you can easily slide the paddle left or right in your hands. If you have to, you can even grasp the throat or blade itself with your "dry" hand. So a shorter paddle is not as limiting as one might think.

Paddle Blade Shape and Size

To determine the blade shape and size look at the type of water you paddle.

If you only do calm, still water (such as quiet, unexposed lakes) a paddle with longer, narrower blades makes sense. These work well with low-angle strokes, catch less water, and offer a less energy-consuming stroke.

If you paddle nothing but faster rivers, you'll want a paddle with short, wide, cupped blades, as they catch the most water and allow the most powerful stroke.

As mentioned in the last section it's more likely you'll encounter a combination of both calm and moving water. And on a river, quick powerful strokes are needed now and then. Therefore, blades that tend towards being shorter, wider, and cupped are recommended for general purpose recreational kayakers.

With your first paddle the blades may be **symmetrical** — the same shape on either side of the center line that's in-line with the paddle shaft. As you improve your skills, you'll want a paddle with **asymmetrical** blades — dissimilar shapes on either side of the center line. (See **Photo 2**.) The top half of the blade is a little larger and longer than the bottom half. This shape is easier to paddle and more efficient. Because of the angle of the paddle when it's in the water, the area of the top and bottom halves becomes equal. So as you pull the paddle through the water it will not try to twist in your hand as experienced with a paddle with symmetrical blades.

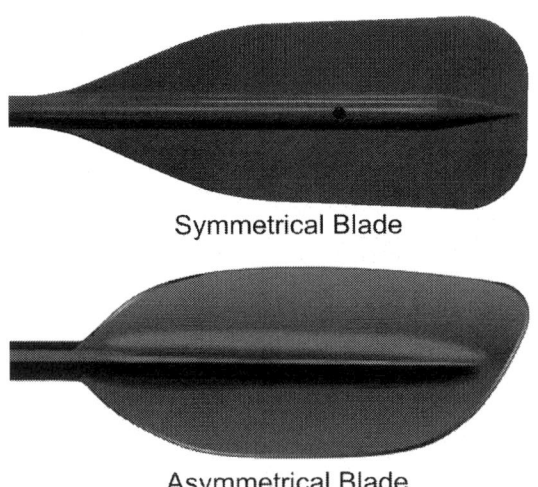

Photo 2 — Symmetrical vs. Asymmetrical Blades

Your first paddle may also be flat. Combined with symmetrical blades, there is no left or right, or up or down, which is very handy for novices. But again, as you improve, it's recommended to go with slightly curved or "cupped" blades which grab the water better. There are also "spoon" shaped blades but these grip the water almost too well, have other issues, and are not recommended.

Regarding blade size, blades with a smaller area catch less water and use less energy and therefore allow a faster cadence. Blades with a larger area catch more water, provide more kayak speed, but require more energy and ultimately fatigue the paddler quicker. So the sea kayaker wants a smaller blade, and the whitewater paddler wants a larger blade. For general purpose recreational kayakers, something in between is recommended.

Paddle Blade Angle: Feathered or Unfeathered?

Sea kayakers typically want a feathered paddle where the blades are not set in the same plane, but are offset by an angle between 45 and 90 degrees, often 60 degrees. Then the blade that's not in the water slices through the air quickly (versus resisting it). A paddle with feathered blades is more efficient and very helpful on long trips on open water. But using it is not intuitive and takes some getting used to. You also have to tilt the wrist of your controlling hand with each and every stroke so it's more likely to cause tendonitis.

As we'll see soon in the "One-piece or Two-piece" section, many two-piece paddles offer the choice of inline or feathered blades as well as the feathering angle. You can also choose between left-hand and right-hand control. With a one-piece paddle the angle between the blades is fixed.

CAUTION: Once you get used to a feathered paddle, switching back to an unfeathered paddle can be dangerous, as you will not be used to the blades in that position. You can go for a bracing stroke and instead slice right through the water encountering no resistance. It's a weird feeling and depending on your situation, you might completely lose your balance!

Feathered paddles are an advantage in headwinds but a slight disadvantage in tailwinds and direct crosswinds.

For recreational kayakers a feathered paddle is not recommended, unless most of the paddling will be on open water and they expect to move up to doing long distance sea-kayak-type trips. Instead, they will be more comfortable with an unfeathered paddle, where the blades in the same plane, that is, where they are "naturally" and "expected" to be. With every stroke, as well as a panic stroke, you do not have to think about if you need to rotate the paddle first. Your reaction will be more intuitive.

Paddle Weight

Reasonable **basic** recreational paddles are typically between 36 and 48 ounces. The heavier paddles may be the basic metal and plastic ones which are the least expensive, very durable, and make good "rentals" as they can take a lot of abuse. Lighter paddles, such as those made with fiberglass or carbon fiber, are much more expensive, require more care, and are not as durable, as the shafts and blades are made of thinner, lighter-weight material. There are also many paddles made with different combinations of materials that are in between for durability, cost, and weight.

Weight is a factor if you are paddling a lot during a trip and/or for a long time. When you move up to a better paddle, though, do not get one so light that it cannot stand up to the typical abuse it will see on the type of water you do most often. Make sure it's durable enough. Usually there's a compromise between weight, durability, and cost.

On the other hand, when choosing your second, better paddle, do not let the cost of a few more dollars stop you from getting a good one. You've spent a lot of time and money on the proper kayak and all the other gear, do not skimp on the paddle. A lighter, stronger, better-designed one versus something less will make all the difference in the enjoyment of the whole paddling experience.

Paddle Shaft and Blade Material

A paddle's shaft and blade material are important factors as well. Shaft material is typically metal, fiberglass, or carbon fiber. Blade material is typically plastic, fiberglass, or carbon fiber. Each has advantages and drawbacks when comparing cost, weight, strength, and durability. For example, a metal shaft is very durable and inexpensive but heavy. A fiberglass or carbon fiber shaft is very light and strong but very expensive. Plastic blades are very durable and inexpensive but heavier. Fiberglass or carbon fiber blades are lighter but not as durable and much more expensive. Also, expect carbon fiber to be more expensive, stronger, and lighter than fiberglass.

Paddle Hand Placement

Generally, the further apart you put your hands the more powerful your stroke. Twice your shoulder width is a good distance for a **power stroke**. For general paddling, shoulder-width apart is way too close — you do not have enough leverage. A good placement for basic paddling is 1.5 times your shoulder width. For example, my shoulder width is 20", so a good distance for relaxed basic paddling is 30". (Thirty inches is also a common distance, center-to-center, that many handles are put on at the factory.) A 40" distance gives me a very good power stroke.

Some suggest a slightly different "normal" position. With the paddle held above your head and your upper arms all the way out to your side, adjust your hands so your upper arms are horizontal and your forearms are perfectly vertical. Measure the distance between your hands, center-to-center. For me that's 34", which is in between a relaxed position (30") and a good power stroke (40").

A common mistake beginners make is putting their hands too close together and/or using a paddle that's too long. This greatly inhibits their leverage so they have a hard time doing almost anything. They are often frustrated yet do not know why.

Tip: Mark the "normal" hand position for you on your paddle in some simple way, such as with duct tape or a permanent marker. Often you may find your hands in the wrong position while paddling so these reference marks can really help.

By the way, a "death grip" on the paddle is not needed or recommended. Instead, maintain a secure but light grip for the most comfort and to prevent overuse injuries.

Paddle Type: One-piece or Two-piece?

When transporting or storing a paddle, having a two-piece (a.k.a. take-apart) paddle is certainly convenient. If you want to change the feathering angle, change between right-hand and left-hand-control, or change to/from unfeathered, this is possible at the **ferrule** (joint) of some two-piece models. The spare paddle I carry is a two-piece — it fits well in the back of the car and inside a kayak. Another feature that can be handy is, if you are stuck in shallow water, a two-piece paddle can be taken apart and each piece used in each hand as "push sticks" to help **scooch** yourself along. My uncle showed us this technique to get over very low beaver dams.

However, two-piece paddles are heavier and generally not as strong as one-piece models. They are fine for your first paddle but when moving up to a better one, consider a one-piece. They can be tied down next to the kayak on racks, or put in your vehicle if you have a station wagon, van, or SUV going from the back end to in between the front seats.

A one-piece paddle will never give the problem of not being able to put the pieces together or take them apart (or accidentally grabbing non-matching pieces if you have more than one — another true story).

Paddle Drip-rings

These are thin rings of rubber around 3" in diameter placed on the paddle shaft just beyond where you put your hands and before the blades. As one blade is dipped in the water and the other is lifted up, the ring on the lifted end stops drips of water from running down the shaft of the paddle, keeping your upper hand dry. This is especially helpful in cold air and/or water. Drip rings should be placed so they do not normally enter the water — so no water comes up with them, or between them and your hands, when the paddle is lifted out of the water.

Note that blade shape effects the amount of water that drips from the blade. At the throat where the edge of the blade joins the shaft, if that angle is shallow, drips can easily run down that edge on to the shaft. If that angle is steep enough, however, the dripping water has to go uphill to get to the shaft, so instead it will drip off of the blade. This can be see in **Photo 2** a few sections back. The angle of the throat on the asymmetrical blade allows less dripping water onto the shaft than the symmetrical blade. (I've improved the blades of some of my cheaper paddles with a belt sander by making the angle of the blade's throat much steeper.)

Paddle Hand Grip: Elliptical or Circular?

A nice feature that's very much recommended is a paddle whose shaft is a slightly different shape from circular at the hand positions. This is accomplished by changing the shape of the shaft or adding material to the shaft, with the result being an elliptically-shaped shaft in the area where your hands normally belong. This has three very helpful advantages:

1. without looking you can tell if your hands are in the right place,
2. without looking you know the orientation of the blades on the paddle, and
3. fingers wrap more comfortably around an elliptical shaft than a circular one.

Two other hand grip considerations are choosing between a slightly bent or straight shaft at the hand positions, and lightly padded or plain hand grips, both of which come down to your personal preference.

Paddle Shaft Diameter

The diameter of a paddle's shaft plays a role in comfort, as well. If the diameter is too small, it can cramp your hands, and if too large, it can cause fatigue in your hands. Your forearms can be affected, as well. Test out different sizes to find one that fits your hands well.

CHOOSING EQUIPMENT — A Quick Summary

The type of water being paddled determines the kayak, paddle, and other gear you should choose. The list below is a very short recap of the recommended equipment based on water type. It will help those new to kayaking as well as experienced paddlers wishing to explore new types of water. Although any kayak and paddle *could be* used on any water, what's shown is the likely *best* choice.

The previous "KAYAK" and "PADDLE" sections provide the complete details about the many choices available.

- Whitewater rivers **Class** III and above (outside of the range of recreational kayaking):
  - Kayak — Whitewater kayak (6' to 8')
  - Paddle — Very short with short, wide blades
- Small, narrow, and twisty recreational rivers:
  - Kayak — Short recreational kayak (9' to 11')
  - Paddle — Short with short, wide blades
- Small to large recreational rivers and close to shore on lakes and bays:
  - Kayak — Medium-sized recreational kayak (12')
  - Paddle — Ideally two paddles — one that's shorter than average with shorter, wider blades for small and medium-sized rivers, and one that's longer than average with longer, narrower blades for lakes and large rivers. If you have to choose just one paddle go with the shorter one.
- Close to shore on lakes, bays, and large recreational rivers:
  - Kayak — Long recreational kayak (13' to 15')
  - Paddle — Long with long, narrow blades
- Open water away from shore (outside of the range of recreational kayaking):
  - Kayak — Touring or sea kayak (16' to 19')
  - Paddle — Long with long, narrow blades

SPRAY SKIRT

Spray skirts are not used with sit-on-top kayaks, so this section applies only to sit-inside kayaks.

A **spray skirt** (a.k.a. spray deck) is a specialized piece of kayak gear made from a waterproof fabric, usually neoprene or coated nylon, that seals around the paddler's chest or waist and the cockpit coaming of the boat. It prevents the kayak from taking in water at the cockpit and has the extra advantage of holding in body heat on colder days.

A spray skirt is absolutely essential for whitewater and sea kayakers because of the rougher conditions they encounter, as well as when leaning, **edging**, and doing **rolls**. (In fact, for these paddlers, at least while still in their boats, a spray skirt could be considered more important than a PFD.)

Recreational kayakers need them too. If they expect to do anything beyond calm water where they might lean significantly (either on purpose as in a deep, edged turn, or by accident if thrown off balance) or encounter waves, bumpy water, or obstacles, a spray skirt is strongly recommended. Without a spray skirt under those conditions it's possible to quickly take in a considerable amount of water, especially on a river if there's much current. That extra water in the boat makes it much more difficult to paddle. If those conditions persist, your kayak could fill with water.

> Note: Without a spray skirt any water taken in the cockpit will need to be emptied at some point. This is easy to do if you stay close to shore (as you should be). If you are out on open water (that is, too far from an accessible shore), you can use a hand-operated **bilge pump** to remove some of the water. But it's often impractical to try to pump out even a half-filled boat. If conditions are favorable and you have the time, bail or pump out what water

you can. Otherwise your best bet is to immediately paddle to shore to empty out your kayak.

> **RECOMMENDATION:** If you are using a sit-inside kayak, a spray skirt is recommended if paddling anything beyond calm water and/or where there are obstacles.

Make sure any spray skirt you buy comes with a **rip cord** (a.k.a. release loop) — a cord or strap at the front of the skirt used to remove it quickly.

WARNING: When attaching the spray skirt be sure the rip cord is hanging out and not tucked in. It's recommended to attach a small plastic whiffle ball to the rip cord, as finding that is much easier and quicker when one is underwater and upside down.

Be sure the "tunnel" of the spray skirt fits well around you and the back of the kayak seat. Make sure the "deck" of the skirt fits and seals well around the coaming. If the spray skirt fits properly, its deck will not easily pop loose from the coaming when you push down hard on it in front of you (simulating a heavy wave splashing in on it). Nor should it come free at the back when you lean far to the side or forward. But it should come off easily when the rip cord is pulled.

Nylon spray skirts are fine for recreational kayakers. They are cheaper, more comfortable, cooler, more adjustable, and easier to get on and off than neoprene versions. Some of these come with a flexible cross-rib that provide an arch in the front which helps the deck of the skirt shed water and makes it less likely to implode.

Whitewater and sea kayakers like neoprene spray skirts because they seal better, are more effective at keeping water out, and therefore are recommended for rolling. But they are more expensive, not as comfortable, and harder to get on and off. Hybrid models are available that have a neoprene deck but an adjustable nylon tunnel. These seal well and are more comfortable than full neoprene models.

As mentioned earlier in the "Kayak Cockpit Size" section, it's much harder to get a spray skirt to seal well or stay in place on a large cockpit. If you'll often be paddling water where a spray skirt is needed, when purchasing a kayak, consider one with a smaller recreational cockpit. A spray skirt on such a cockpit seals better and is much less likely to implode when a wave lands directly on the deck of the skirt. Also make sure a spray skirt is available that fits the kayak well.

By the way, a spray skirt also helps when one tips over. That is, if one has thigh braces, stays in the boat, and knows how to roll. But that's not likely for the vast majority of recreational kayakers. So in the event of a capsize and **wet exit**, an **open-water rescue** will be needed, which is something the average recreational kayaker will not know how to do. Even if one did, he/she would still need to bail most of the water using a hand-operated bilge pump, which can take quite a lot of time. One's best option is to swim and push/pull the swamped kayak to shore — not easily done. All of which emphasizes why **CARDINAL RULE IV** for recreational kayakers is that they should never venture far from an accessible shore.

LIFE JACKET / PFD

> **RECOMMENDATION:** Always wear a life jacket. (The life you save will be your own and allow you to help others.)

The single most important piece of safety equipment a paddler possesses is a brain, specifically the ability to make the proper choices needed to avoid or lessen the severity of a potential mishap.

Following that a life jacket is for sure the next most important — in the event of leaving one's boat while on the water. A life jacket is required for anyone using a kayak. If you are not going to wear one, or at least have one with you, do not operate a kayak (or any boat).

The life jacket you wear should be a USCG-approved Type III (or better, if needed) PFD — personal floatation device.

- A Type I PFD is recommended for rough, open water where a rescue may be slow in coming. It WILL turn an unconscious person face-up in the water.

- A Type II PFD is recommended for calm, open water but close to shore where a rescue is expected soon. It may or may not turn an unconscious person face-up in the water.

- A Type III life jacket is for calm water where rescue is expected soon. It usually will NOT turn an unconscious person face-up.

A Type III life jacket is all most recreational kayakers need. They are less bulky, more comfortable, and less expensive than Types I and II.

A life jacket is only of any good if it's being worn, and will likely only be worn if it's comfortable. Get a life vest model that's designed for kayakers which has narrow shoulder straps and plenty of open room around the shoulders for arm movement. It should be no longer than waist length to accommodate a spray skirt. The bottom of the back should be high enough to not hit the back of the kayak seat. Make sure it fits around you snugly so it will not "ride up" on you when in the water. Lift it up at the shoulders and make sure it stays in place. But, it should not be so tight that it's hard to breath or uncomfortable to paddle. Test the life jacket by sitting with it on while in your kayak and going through all your normal paddling motions. It's recommended to test it while in the water, too!

Two handy features to look for on a life jacket are self-draining pockets and lash pads to which you can attach accessories, such as a whistle.

Although the USCG (United States Coast Guard), some states and provinces, and/or local laws and ordinances require the paddler to wear a life jacket when operating a kayak on certain bodies of water, not all locations have that requirement. Regardless, there must always be a life jacket on board for everyone occupying the boat. Any children must ALWAYS wear a life jacket. Even if you are not required to wear one, it is **strongly recommended**. When in the water, it's way too difficult to find the life jacket, remove it from the kayak, and put it on, usually under adverse circumstances.

If you are allowed to not wear a life jacket and choose, instead, to stow it in/on your kayak:

- Never, ever stow a life jacket in the hatch of a sit-inside kayak. It's way too difficult to access while in the water and during the process the compartment will flood and likely some of the cockpit.

- Never stow a life jacket loose in/on your kayak, such as for a backrest or down by your feet. Should you tip over it will be one of the first things to float away and perhaps get lost, especially if you are on a river, in rough water, or there's considerable wind. (If you need a backrest or seat cushion, whatever you use, make sure it's tied to the boat somehow or is something you can afford to sacrifice.)

- You *can* stow the life jacket behind the seat of a sit-inside kayak IF you have a stern bulkhead, as this keeps the PFD from traveling to the rear of the boat, keeps it in place when you capsize, and makes it relatively easy to pull it out. But make sure it cannot float away if you capsize.

- It's *best* to put the life jacket under cargo lines on the deck or top-side as it will stay in place if you tip over and is in the easiest place to access.

- Make sure you are very fast and skilled at taking the life jacket off the boat and putting it on. (Note that *no one* is really that fast and skilled in any real-life situation.)

In addition, never use your life jacket as a seat cushion, kneeling pad, or in any way that flattens out the foam inside. That will cause it to lose buoyancy.

When not in use, dry out your PFD then store it in a dry, well-ventilated space, out of any sunlight. Inspect it at least once a year and test it in water, as well. Does it still do its job properly? If there's any doubt, replace it. Take it apart so it does not ever get accidentally used again as a life jacket.

CLOTHING

> **RECOMMENDATION:** Consider your clothing carefully. Always dress and prepare for going in the water. Be aware of the expected temperature of the water you are about to paddle.

A lot of less-experienced kayakers dress for the weather. That's fine, a good start, but wrong. One should **always prepare and dress for going and being in the water (CARDINAL RULE III)**. Wear the appropriate clothes for both getting cold and getting wet. Be aware of the expected water temperature. Consider how long you might be in the water and how long before you will be able to get into dry clothes.

Remember, with a sit-on-top kayak, expect at least some parts of you will be wet much of the trip (part of the fun, right?!), so dress accordingly. In any kayak you will be very exposed to the sun, so on a strong sunny day put on plenty of sunscreen and/or wear lightweight, quick-drying pants and a long-sleeved shirt.

Clothing Basics

Cotton is very comfortable but very bad when wet because it holds moisture and takes a long time to dry. Wool keeps you warm even when wet, but it gets heavy, can be constricting, and dries very slowly. Much better is quick-drying, waterproof, synthetic material.

Dress in layers so you can easily remove or put on clothing as needed. For your first layer wear clothes that wick moisture away from the body, such as polypropylene. Fleece is a good second layer as it insulates even when wet but does not restrict movement. The outside layer needs to protect against wind and water. Lightweight, waterproof but breathable fabric is best.

If the water is cold enough (50 degrees Fahrenheit or less), it's recommended to wear a shortie neoprene **wet** suit under your clothes. Without a wet suit, at least wear an outer layer of a **spray top** and **paddling pants**.

Wear a swimsuit only if both the air and water temperatures are warm enough and will stay that way for the duration of the trip. Another option is a light top and quick-drying nylon shorts.

Do not wear bulky jackets, ponchos, heavy boots, waders, or anything else which could reduce your ability to survive "swimming" in the water to the nearest accessible shore after a capsize.

Dry Clothes

For trips of any considerable length, you should always bring along a full set of dry clothes. Keep these in a **dry bag** and stowed inside a watertight compartment if possible. A pack towel is recommended, as well, so you can dry off before putting on the dry clothes. Having a second set of dry clothes in your vehicle in not a bad idea, either, in case the first set gets wet.

Jacket

Bring a fleece jacket or equivalent — it's very handy if you get chilly and/or the wind picks up. Keep it easy to access.

Rain Gear

If there's any chance of rain, bring rain gear along, both rain jacket and pants. Include a waterproof rain hat with a sturdy brim that will keep your head dry and warm and shed the water. Make sure it has a strap to hold it in place for when it's windy. Keep all raingear easy to access.

Hat

A wide-brimmed hat made from waterproof, quick-drying material is recommended for keeping you cool and the sun out of your eyes and off your head, face, and neck.

It's also nice if it starts to rain. Make sure it has a strap to hold it in place for when it's windy.

In strong sunshine even with such a hat you should still put on sunscreen as the sun will reflect off the water and under the brim of the hat.

When the weather is cool and cloudy, a light wool, or better yet, synthetic (such as fleece) cap will help hold in the heat even when wet.

Any hat you wear will also be helpful on a river when going through brush or overhanging trees.

Sunglasses

Polarized sunglasses are recommended as they greatly reduce the glare on the water, protect your eyes, and allow you to see obstacles in the water and the bottom much more clearly. (See also "Glasses" below.)

Glasses

For ANY glasses you wear, be sure you have a strap on them. You can easily get bumped and lose the glasses in the water, not to mention what happens if you capsize! Consider bringing along a spare pair of glasses on long trips (especially any multi-day venture).

Footwear

If you wear shoes or sandals, and usually you should, be sure they are waterproof or ones you do not mind getting wet. They should be lightweight and not bulky. When used in a sit-inside kayak make sure they fit well inside and are easy to get in and out of place. They should be comfortable when wet. Look at the types of shore you might be encountering to be sure the shoes can accommodate all of them, such as slippery rocks, sharp rocks and shells, sandy beach, thick mud, logs and branches, wild woods, dense foliage, etc. You may also have to get out in the water — can your shoes stand up to the types of bottom of the body of water you'll be on? At any time will you have to walk with or without your boat on land? How far? Can your shoes handle whatever you'll be walking on, including sharp rocks, or even broken glass?

Some kayakers like Crocs (or similar) because they are lightweight, waterproof, and have a good sole. Get the kind with a heel strap so they stay in place when walking in water or mud.

An old pair of sneakers (a.k.a. tennis shoes, gym shoes, running shoes, etc.) will work if the soles are not too bulky. But once wet they may stay wet for a long time. Be sure to tuck in the ends and loops of the laces so they cannot catch on anything, especially foot rests.

Flip flops are not recommended as they come off when walking in water or mud and can get hung up on foot rests.

Beware of sandals with straps — the straps on some types can catch on foot rests, such as during a **wet exit**.

Thin little slip-on "water slippers" are "okay" but they come off too easily especially in muddy river banks, provide no arch support, and have relatively meager bottoms for protection.

Recreational paddlers should avoid big rubber boots. Sure, they offer good foot protection and keep your feet dry (in very shallow water, anyway). However, they are way too heavy and bulky and can easily get trapped inside a kayak. And should they become flooded with water they effectively become anchors making them very dangerous. The same is also true for hip boots, even fishing waders.

A common choice is good pair water shoes or sandals during warm periods, then add neoprene, wool, fleece, or other waterproof and breathable socks for cooler times. Or go with neoprene booties — they are similar to neoprene socks but zip on and off, come with thick rubber soles, yet are not bulky like shoes or sandals.

Note that all of these recommended footwear ideas protect your feet, some help keep your feet warm, but none keep your feet completely dry. So it's nice to have a pair of dry socks and comfy sneakers ready and waiting at the end of the trip.

Gloves

Warm and waterproof gloves (such as neoprene) are needed if the water and/or air temperatures are cold. If both are warm, some paddlers like lightweight synthetic paddling gloves (or those used by water skiers or cyclists), especially if they are prone to blisters. Other paddlers like fingerless gloves. Certain types of gloves may provide a better grip, such as those with rubber-coated palms used by fisherman. In warmer conditions gloves may not be needed, especially if the hand grips are padded. When it's warmer, I prefer to not wear gloves as I like the more "positive" feel of direct hand-to-paddle contact.

OTHER GEAR

After kayaking for over 30 years one learns what's helpful to have along on a trip, especially longer river trips with a group. Below are a few lists compiled from my own experience, that of fellow paddlers, and recommended by others "in the business".

> **RECOMMENDATION:** "Know before you go" and prepare well beforehand so you bring along the appropriate gear.

Good things to know before you go:

- Yourself, your needs and abilities.

- Your boat. (Know, know, know your boat, gently 'cross the sea...!)

- The water you are about to paddle, its current and expected conditions, and its temperature.

- The environment of shoreline of the water you'll be on, such as rocky, thick woods, sandy beach, swampy, or wild and rugged.

- If you be able to land anywhere along the way.

- If there people or any services available at the put-in and take-out points and along the way.

- When will you eat — before, during, and after the trip.

- If there restrooms available.

- The expected weather. (Are you prepared if the prediction is wrong?)

- The expected length of the trip.

Knowing all of these will help you be as prepared as possible. Then use the following lists to fully "arm" yourself and those with you with the appropriate gear. Add to these lists anything missing that's needed for your particular needs.

Gear Each Person Should Bring

- cell phone
- drinking water
- life jacket or PFD
- snacks and/or food for meals
- good, loud storm/safety whistle
- full set of dry clothes in a dry bag
- rain jacket — if there's any chance of rain
- sunscreen — reapply as needed on longer trips or after any swimming
- anything needed for outdoor restroom stops — toilet paper and disinfectant wipes, for sure
- car keys — both a main set and spare set if you are a driver on the trip. Consider swapping the spare set with another driver. If you leave your wallet or spare keys somewhere safe before the trip, tell others, or at least the leader of the group.

Gear Each Person Should Consider Bringing

- watch
- camera
- binoculars
- spare paddle
- insect repellent
- polarized sunglasses
- light fleece jacket or equivalent
- good rain gear (hat, jacket, pants)
- spray skirt — if the conditions warrant it
- rope for pulling kayak through shallow water
- guide books (or apps) to local flora and/or fauna
- waterproof covering to keep your legs dry and warm
- a towel to prevent sunburn on your legs (sit-inside kayak)
- first aid kit (especially for many different types of cuts) in a **dry bag** or **dry box**
- other drinking liquids if desired besides water (but no alcohol — save that for later)
- a second set of clothes, socks, shoes, and a towel in your vehicle for the end of the trip

- additional food such as fruit, dried fruit, energy bars, Granola bars, beef jerky (bring something fun to share, too!)
- floatable seat pads, back cushions, etc. (Hopefully your seat is comfortable enough without anything extra as loose things are too easily lost should you tip over.)

Gear Group Leaders Should Consider Bringing

- watch
- lighter
- compass
- flashlight
- binoculars
- GPS device
- spare paddle
- marine radio
- small tree saw
- spare life jacket
- Swiss Army knife
- multi-purpose tool
- emergency blanket
- general purpose rope
- aspirin, Motrin, Benadryl
- road map of the local area
- **throw bag** and rescue knife
- a map app on a smart phone
- rescue and emergency equipment
- spare batteries for any electronics
- waterproof matches or fire-starter
- spare clothes to share, kept in a **dry bag**
- waterproof "walkie-talkie" two-way radios
- weather radio (or radio that includes an **NWR** band)
- tow line — 25' or longer, to tow a **swimmer** or a kayaker
- **nautical chart** of the water being done, or at least a detailed map
- duct tape, **Magic Patch**, and other boat repair material and tools
- method(s) for bailing water: bilge pump (or two), bailer, sponges, towels, etc.

- first aid kit (especially for cuts, both long & lean and short & mean) in a **dry bag** or **dry box**
- lotions and potions to prevent and minimize the result from bee strings, bugs bites, poison ivy, leeches, snake bites, swelling, ticks, etc.
- **paddle float** — but only if you and your group is trained in its use. This presumes you are going out in open water beyond what's recommended for recreational kayakers.

> **RECOMMENDATION:** Stow your gear well — it's only any good if it stays with you. Make sure any gear that needs to stay dry is in a waterproof **dry bag** or **dry box** as well as a in a watertight hatch, if present, and if not, well-secured to the kayak.

Stowing Gear

- Be sure that anything that should not get wet is stowed in a **dry bag** or **dry box** as well as in a watertight compartment, if available.
- Be especially sure cell phones, cameras, and other electronics are protected in a **dry box**. Some people go even farther and put them in a Ziploc bag, as well.
- If you bring your wallet with you — some people feel it's safest to do so — be sure it is well-protected from getting wet or lost if you tip over.
- Make sure all gear is well-secured and protected from getting lost if you tip over. Anything loose will float away carried by the current, waves, or wind. Ideally your helpers will only have to go after just three things — you, your boat, and your paddle — and not a "laundry list" of all the extra stuff you brought along.
- Keep some things you'll need while paddling within easy reach, such as a jacket, drinking water, camera, snacks, sunscreen, and rain gear.

IV. RULES and GENERAL RECOMMENDATIONS

> **RECOMMENDATION:** Please study and follow the rules and recommendations presented here. Disobey them at your own risk.

CARDINAL KAYAKING RULES

Before you go on any kayak trip there are four cardinal rules you need to be aware of that absolutely must be followed. The first three apply to ALL KAYAKERS not just recreational kayakers. No one enforces these other than nature and fate!

- **RULE I. Never put yourself into any situation from which you cannot easily recover.** (Perhaps a good lesson for life as well.) Use common sense. If you have any real doubt, don't do it. Please burn this into your brain. This is how a great many mishaps occur, even for experts. Part of this is being aware of the **many things you should know** covered in the following "GENERAL KAYAKING RECOMMENDATIONS" section.

- **RULE II. Always paddle with at least one other person, never paddle alone.** But if you insist on doing this, please at least make sure that you:
  - never, ever paddle a river alone.
  - never, ever paddle exposed water alone, but always with at least one other experienced paddler. (Exposed water is that in which you are vulnerable to hazards from which you cannot recover, such as open water with wind, waves, and current, and may also include being too far from shore. Know that conditions can change quickly on exposed water.)
  - have notified some responsible person as to exactly when and where you expect to start and finish (so they can at least rescue the kayak!!).

- o have taken a kayak rescue and safety course.
- o are proficient at **self-rescue** and can easily rescue yourself from any situation that comes up, especially unexpected circumstances.
- o take a cell phone — hopefully you'll have service and any rescuers, if they find you, do not arrive too late.
- o are extra careful, much more so than if you were not alone, and obey RULES I, III, and IV.
- o are aware that there are potential situations from which you might not recover.
- o are prepared for and willing to accept any consequences.

- **RULE III. Always prepare and dress for going and being in the water.** Be sure you know...
  - o you are wearing a life jacket.
  - o the temperature of the water in which you are about to paddle.
  - o if you go in the water, how long you are likely to be in it before you are rescued, rescue yourself, or swim to an accessible shore.
  - o how far you will have to swim to shore.
  - o that you have dry clothes available when you reach shore.
  - o what the weather conditions are — temperature, wind, rain, fog, and sun.
  - o you are prepared and dressed appropriately for all of the above.
  - o that not being properly prepared could lead to the dangerous condition of **hypothermia**.

- **RULE IV. Recreational kayakers — always stay close to an accessible shore** so you can easily paddle or swim to it, especially if your boat is filled with water and/or you have to drag it with you. This applies to open water, lakes larger than perhaps 40 acres, slow but very wide rivers, and any river with a fast current that's more than perhaps 100 feet wide.

(This is really a specific case of **RULE I**, but it's important enough that is deserves to be on its own.)

Please teach these rules and GENERAL KAYAKING RECOMMENDATIONS that follow to any and all kayakers you know. Everyone will benefit from these. Ideally have them read this book!

GENERAL KAYAKING RECOMMENDATIONS

The following are highly recommended for all kayakers on any type of water...

Before the trip...

- There are **many things you should know** before going on any trip which will help you be as prepared (and therefore relaxed) as possible.

    o Know yourself, your abilities, needs, and requirements.

    o Know your boat, what it can handle and what it cannot.

    o Know the water you are about to paddle, its depth and expected conditions. For a river, know its current height, speed, **gradient**, and **classification**. Be aware that conditions can change quickly, especially on larger, less-protected, more-exposed bodies of water.

    o Know the expected temperature of the water, both at the surface and six feet down, if possible. Be prepared for being in it for a considerable length of time. With water colder than 60 degrees Fahrenheit the risk factor begins to go up considerably. With water 50 degrees or colder a wet suit should be worn. Some experts recommend not paddling if the water temperature is 55 degrees or less and you do not have cold-water paddling gear.

- Know any expected impediments, obstacles, and/or obstructions on the water you are about to paddle.
- Know the expected boat traffic where you will be paddling.
- Know the types of environment of the shoreline or banks of the water you'll be paddling and if and where it's accessible.
- Know the planned and any alternate access sites to the water you'll be paddling.
- Know if there are any people or services available at the **put-in** and **take-out** points as well as along the way.
- Know the exact take-out point of the trip and what to watch for to locate it from the water.
- Know when will you eat — before, during, and after the trip.
- Know if and where restrooms are available.
- Know the expected weather during the trip, especially the predicted wind. Are you prepared if the prediction is wrong?
- Know to avoid paddling if there's any chance of lightning, NOTE: If you are already on the water and hear thunder and/or the possibility of lightning arises, get off the water NOW. You are a very attractive target for lightning especially on open water.
- Know to avoid paddling if the fog is so thick that you would not easily see the shore or river bank when paddling a few hundred feet from it. Wait for a while — if it's morning, the sun or wind of midday may burn or blow it away.
- Know that you are prepared for common surprises, such as wind and/or waves picking up on more

open water, and unexpected tree-fall, obstacles, and portages on rivers.

- Know that you prepared for at least the most common unexpected surprises.

- Know that anyone can tip over at any time — no one is immune — and it's often unpredictable. Are you prepared for this and are others prepared to help?

- Know the people you are paddling with to some degree. What's their general temperament, paddling and swimming ability, if they have any expertise, special needs, etc. It helps if you know at least one person well. Try to meet everyone going and learn at least their first names.

- Ideally you should **be able to swim** or at the bare minimum be able to tread water well.

- You should be one who is **not afraid** of being in a boat, being on or in the water, getting wet, and capsizing. (It's not that you will capsize on any given trip, but do not be afraid of it, and be dressed and prepared for it.) Be aware of the most common possibilities and how to handle them so you are not be overly fearful about them. The knowledge and understanding gained from this book should help dispel fears and hopefully allow you to be relaxed and enjoy yourself.

- **Never, ever drag any kayak** across any rough surface such as gravel, concrete, and asphalt, but only on soft surfaces such as sand, grass, soft dirt, or firm mud. Dragging it on any rough surface will scrape up the bottom and begin to wear it away. Dragging a kayak on its tail is a super "no-no" as doing so will quickly wear through the boat's material, which can break through when least expected and leave a hole that's very difficult to repair.

Leaders...

- **If you are choosing the water to be paddled**, take into account most of the "many things you should know" just mentioned, especially the type of water. Make sure all paddlers participating and all aspects of the trip are suitable for each other.

- Besides never paddling alone (CARDINAL RULE II), it's best to **have a minimum of three people on any trip**. If one person gets in trouble the second person can aid the first while the third person can rescue the kayak and paddle, assist in a tricky rescue, and/or go for help. Some recommend a minimum of five people on any paddling trip.

- It helps to keep the group to around **ten people or less**, as that's an easy number of people to manage and communicate with. If you have a large number going at once, consider dividing into more manageable sub-groups.

- Create a **trip plan** — where and when to meet ahead of time, the exact put-in and take-out points. start and end times, specific paddle route, and expected stops along the way for meals and breaks. Be sure everyone knows the plan beforehand.

- Make sure that at least one responsible person not on the trip has been made aware of the trip plan and the names of everyone on the trip.

- Any paddling trip should also include an **emergency plan** in case of any serious medical emergency. That plan should include:
    - Bringing along the proper first aid kit for all common paddling injuries and issues.
    - Knowing the medical condition of all of those on the trip.

- o   Knowing if anyone has any health concerns or special needs and what's required should they need help.
- o   Having the phone number of the emergency contact for each person on the trip.
- o   Knowing if any in the group are trained medical professionals.
- o   Bringing a well-charged cell phone and knowing if there will be cell phone service.
- o   Knowing the nearest access site at any point along the trip.
- o   Knowing what if any emergency services are available at those access sites.
- o   At any point on the trip, knowing how many hours away are you from emergency services.
- o   Knowing the location of the nearest hospital and/or urgent care facility.

• Before heading out on a trip, have a general idea of how vehicles will be **shuttled**. Then when everyone meets with vehicles and boats, work out the exact **shuttle plan** for before and after the trip. You do not want any surprises!

• Do what you can to **discourage the use of any alcohol** both before and during the trip. Save that for after the trip. Alcohol leads to making poor decisions and decreases the ability to act on any decision. Whether saving themselves or helping to save others, you need everyone to be as sober, sharp, and in control as possible. Alcohol is also detrimental to those who might experience **heat stroke** or **hypothermia** during the trip. A "no alcohol" policy is best.

On the trip...

- Be sure you are always prepared for the possibility of **taking on** and **going in the water**.

- In cool or cold air, it's important to stay warm, dry, hydrated, well-fed, and not become over-tired. Avoid any alcohol. Not doing these can lead to **hypothermia**. Keep an extra layer of clothing, water, and a snack within easy reach.

- On a hot day in direct sun, especially when exerting yourself over an extended period of time (such as on a long paddle trip), it's important to stay cool, protected from the sun, hydrated, well-fed, and not become over-tired. Avoid any alcohol. Not doing these can lead to **heat stroke**. Wear light-colored, loose-fitting clothing and keep water and a snack within easy reach.

- **Take breaks.** Sitting in the same position continually is usually hard on the body. Shift positions occasionally, as much as your kayak will allow. On longer trips pull over and get out once an hour to stretch, bend, take a quick walk, etc. to undo any tension and knots that may have built up. While sitting on land with your legs out in front of you, do some hamstring stretches and torso rotations. This is also a good time for a restroom stop and light snack. Breaks are especially important if you are exerting yourself on a long trip as they give you a chance to relax. When the air is cool or cold, drink something warm or hot and walk around a little. On hot days and/or longer trips it's important to drink plenty of water or Gatorade-type of drinks.

- Don't be afraid to **call for a break**. Folks new to kayaking are exercising muscles not normally used so they become fatigued more easily. The chances are good that other paddlers will welcome a break as well for one reason or another.

- On a regular basis, such as on any break and at the beginning and end of every trip, **check for water inside** the hull and all the "watertight" compartments. Water can and will find its way in via any number of unexpected ways, such as loose hatch covers and drain plugs, leaking bulkheads, and cracks in a hull seam. This applies to both sit-inside and sit-on-top kayaks. (It's sneakier with sit-on-top kayaks because they can take on water without your knowledge, as it's not easy to see what's inside the hull.) Remove or drain out the water as needed. A sponge or **bilge pump** can be used for small amounts of water. If there's a lot, roll the boat on its side, turn it upside down, rock it back and forth, etc. Fix any leaking issues, if possible. Be aware of any leaks you cannot fix at the moment to address later in the day.

- Have everyone **carry a good safety whistle**, one that's loud and can be heard at a great distance (such as the Fox 40 or Storm). These are required by law on some bodies of water and are a good idea anyway.

  It's very convenient to hang the whistle around your neck so it's easy find when needed. However, if you go in the water on a river there's a chance the lanyard can get caught on a branch or tree (which might be the cause of why you are in the water in the first place). So, unless the whistle is on a break-away lanyard it's much safer to attach it to your life jacket.

  Make sure everyone knows the calls you'll be using before heading out...
  - A long blast typically means: *I just need everyone's attention*. Everyone should stop and listen for further instructions.
  - Three short blasts usually means: *Things are very serious. I need help, now!* Everyone should stop and attend to the person in trouble, as needed.
  - For what it's worth, three short blasts, three long, then three short is the universal SOS call. (It's

Morse code for S-O-S.) But that's way too much to do when you are in trouble.

- Use **paddle signals**. Better than shouting and more communicative than a whistle, these are very effective when there is a group and especially useful on more challenging rivers. If you are without a paddle you can use your arms. Be sure the paddle blades are facing the people you are signaling (usually those behind or upstream of you). Make sure everyone knows the signals you'll be using before heading out. When you see a paddle signal pass the word along to those upstream.

  Some paddle signals common to North America are:

  o **STOP** — Hold your paddle horizontally over your head. To grab everyone's attention raise and lower it quickly several times. This means: *everyone is to stop in place and not go past the person signaling. There is some form of hazard ahead. Proceed only once a further signal is given, such as ALL CLEAR or THIS WAY.*

  A good time to use this is when someone ahead is hung up in a river passage that everyone must go through. The STOP signal, given by the next person in line, keeps everyone from piling up on the person in trouble.

  Note: Doing this signal along with a long blast on your whistle will help grab the attention of those nearby.

  o **HELP** — Wave an end of your paddle (or arms or a life jacket) over your head, ideally along with three short blasts of your whistle, or at least shout out, "Help, help, help!". This signal is an *urgent call for help — everyone who can should immediately come to the aid of the signaller.* Do not be shy — it's better to get attention and perhaps not need it after all than the converse of needing assistance with no one around to help.

- **ALL CLEAR** — Hold your paddle at rest vertically over your head with the blade facing the people you are signaling. This means: *it's now safe to come on ahead.* You may need to follow this with a THIS WAY signal directing people to one side of the river.

- **THIS WAY** — Begin with an ALL CLEAR signal, then tilt the paddle down to 45 degrees in the recommended direction of travel (**river left** or **river right**) holding it there a moment. To grab everyone's attention, repeat this signal several times. Do it slowly and deliberately making sure it does not look like you are waving the paddle or it could be confused with the HELP signal.

- **I'M OK** — not done with a paddle — hold your elbow far out to your side and repeatedly tap yourself on the head, This tells folks: *I am OK and do not require an help,* and perhaps: *I am ready to go.*

  This can also start as a question. If someone looking at you then points directly at you and taps their head, they are asking, "Are you OK?!" If you are OK immediately tap your head a few times in response. If you do not, it's presumed you are in trouble and need help — the person asking is to come to your rescue.

- **PULLING OFF THE RIVER** — meaning: *we are temporarily landing for some reason (lunch, a break, to portage, scout ahead, whatever).* No commonly accepted signal exists, so I suggest each group make up their own.

  I propose using a combination of the THIS WAY and STOP signals. While pointing to the side of the river on which the landing is occurring, start with a THIS WAY signal pointing one end of the paddle up at 45 degrees, then lower it to the horizontal STOP signal, holding it there a moment. Repeat several times as needed.

- When **paddling before sunrise or after sunset** make sure you have a good flashlight, white lantern, or fixed light in full display. (The laws for some bodies of water may require even more, such as flares and/or an electric distress light.) To make yourself more visible, consider adding reflective tape to the front and back faces of your paddle's blades, perhaps on your PFD, and along the gunwale of your kayak. Also, a headlamp will help you be seen both in the dark and during foggy conditions.

- Be very careful when **paddling anywhere near** a steep shore or bank, seawall, concrete pier, bridge piling, or similar structure as waves bouncing (*rebounding*) off of these mixes with waves coming in creating a confusion of turbulent water.

- **When someone capsizes** and goes in the water, be honorable and **take no photos**. If you are that close you should be helping out in some way, anyway.

- A few **simple reminders**: As you explore the various waterways of the world you will often be alongside private property — never access it without permission. Please be respectful of all land you travel upon or nearby being careful to leave it unharmed. Do not disturb any live plants, trees, or wildlife. Certainly feed no wildlife. Never leave or bury any food waste or litter but take it all with you. Tread lightly and with respect, behaving as you would have others act if they visited where you live, work, and play. Be one of Nature's stewards leaving it unharmed and available to be experienced and appreciated by all who follow.

V. PADDLING

Now the fun can begin...!

If you are new to kayaking, on a nice day in warm water on a small, calm lake or the still water at the edge of a very calm river, take the time to learn and practice the basic strokes and maneuvers in the following "EXPLORING THE BASICS" section.

If you have just acquired a new (or new-to-you) kayak and are familiar with the basics, try it out as covered in the upcoming "TESTING YOUR KAYAK" section. Read through the following "EXPLORING THE BASICS" section as it's likely you will learn some things you did not already know. Ideally go through the steps involved as a refresher.

EXPLORING THE BASICS

> **RECOMMENDATION:** If you are new to kayaking, before heading out on any real trip take the time to learn and practice the basic paddling strokes and maneuvers. If you are not new to kayaking, go through these as a refresher.

Before Launching

Before getting on the water, set things up for comfort and good posture — it's much easier doing so beforehand than when on the water.

Adjust the foot rests so that, with the balls of your feet on the foot rests (pedal type), your legs are gently apart in a comfortable position and your knees are slightly bent. Also so that (with some sit-inside kayaks) your knees or thighs are able to comfortably but snugly "lock" in place against the side, under the edge of the cockpit opening. or in the thigh braces of the boat.

Adjust the seat's backrest so you are sitting upright and your back is well supported. Make any other adjustments now for a comfortable position.

If you will be using a spray skirt, put it on before putting on your life jacket and before entering the kayak. Once in the boat and just before launching, attach the skirt to the coaming. It's much easier to do so now than when on the water.

Tips for Launching and Landing

As you enter and exit your kayak, unless it's on firm ground, do not stand up. Keep your center of gravity as low as possible while keeping your hands on both sides of the cockpit area for balance. In wobbly situations ask someone for help to hold the boat steady.

Try to launch and land where there's a shallow incline of sand, grass, dirt, and/or firm mud entering the water. Try to avoid any gravel, and never launch or land at an asphalt, concrete, or cement-block ramp unless it's an emergency. Often on the side of a hard-surface boat ramp is a bit of dirt, sand, or light gravel. You want a smooth entry into the water and want to avoid scraping the bottom anymore than absolutely necessary,

When launching, go in stern-end first, perpendicular to the shore. If you are lucky and the water is deep enough, you can keep the cockpit close to the shore and not even get your feet wet. If the water is too shallow you will have to put the cockpit out a little ways from the water's edge.

Once you are sitting in the kayak, while pushing gently on the lake/river bottom with your paddle and mostly by **scooching** (and maybe a little **knuckle walking**), carefully slide into the water. It certainly helps if other paddlers still onshore can give you a push or two.

By going in stern first, there's much less drag on the part of the boat that's still on land, so it's easier for the kayak to slide into the water. It's also more stable and smoother if there is any kind of little ledge at the water's edge or the bank tends towards the steeper side. (If this is the case, brace carefully with your paddle, because midway along, with one end of the kayak afloat and the other teetering on shore, you are quite vulnerable to tipping over.) Launching stern first also lessens the pressure and scraping on the stern keel, the area of the hull that gets the most wear.

If launching from the shore is not practical, take the kayak out to about 3" to 4" of water where there's firm but not rocky bottom. Straddle the cockpit, drop yourself in seat-first, then bring in your legs. With sit-on-top boats and wider sit-insides you can also just "plop" in from the side. Experiment a little to see what technique works best for you and your kayak. Once most of your weight is in the boat it should gently touch bottom giving you a bit of stability as you get situated. From here it's easy to scooch and push yourself to get underway.

Launching and landing through waves at the shore of a lake or ocean is not covered as those conditions are beyond **recreational kayak water** and requires skills beyond recreational kayaking.

To land, ideally there will be a lake shore or river bank at a shallow enough angle that you can just run up onto it fast, then scooch a bit to get close to the water's edge. The first person to land may get his/her feet wet, but then he/she can help pull the others up as they land.

Or, you may be able to land parallel to the shore then lean the kayak into it and/or onto the lake/river bottom for stability as you exit the boat.

If you are not so fortunate, you may need to just go as close as you can to shore and get out in the water. Anyone who has landed already can lend a hand. (And if they are not soaking wet from a failed attempt, ask them how they landed — they may have found a better approach.)

Basic Strokes and Maneuvers

Going Forward

For the basic forward stroke, you just plunk the paddle down in the water in front of where you are sitting on one side of the kayak and pull backwards, right? Um, nope, sorry. Paddling this way, you are using just your arms and shoulders. If you did this a long time you would become tired and sore and your shoulders may start to burn.

Instead, begin by sitting up straight with a good posture then twist your upper body to one side, extend your arm on that side, and at a point even with your feet put the paddle's blade fully in the water. Then unwind and twist your upper body in the other direction, pushing slightly with your top arm and resist pulling with your bottom arm, moving the blade backwards parallel to the keel of the boat. Finish by removing the blade once it goes past your hips. You are now in position to paddle on the other side of the kayak.

Done properly, you are not pulling the paddle with your bottom arm as much as you are pushing with your top arm as your body rotates. The less pulling you do the gentler you are on your arms and shoulders and will get fewer blisters.

Paddling this way your arms bend relatively little. You are using larger and longer upper torso muscle groups so your strokes are more powerful and efficient yet less fatiguing. Says a kayaking friend, "your paddling power is then coming from your core". A beginner's trick which helps facilitate the needed upper body rotation is to keep your eye on the blade that's in the water as you go through the motion of the stroke.

When making this stroke (or any stroke) use only enough force to get the job done. Many beginners start out paddling too hard. Then they try to over compensate on the opposite side and wind up going in a wild serpentine pattern. Instead, try to develop a smooth technique, paddling consistently with just an easy to moderate effort. Use an equal force on both sides in a steady rhythm.

Practice moving forward with smooth and easy left and right strokes, keeping the boat going straight at a steady pace. If needed, make small course corrections by just paddling a little harder or easier on one side and/or putting the paddle a bit closer to or further from the kayak.

A tip that helps one to go straight is to not look at the bow of the boat but instead focus on a fixed object onshore. In just a little time you'll find you automatically stop over-correcting and start making minor course corrections by adjusting how close or far out you place the paddle as well as how hard you paddle.

As you gain experience you can use the following technique to improve the efficiency of your stroke. It's done by pushing on the foot rest on the side on which you are paddling. With your feet are on the foot rests, as you twist at the beginning of the forward stroke, just before you plant the blade in the water, your leg on that side (called the **on-stroke** side) will be bent slightly more and pressing harder on the foot rest. Your leg on the other side (the **off-stroke** side) will be slightly more extended with less pressure on the foot rest. As you carry out the stroke, unwinding then twisting the other way, push with your off-stroke leg until at the end of the stroke. The situation with your legs will now be the reverse of what it was at the beginning of the stroke. Doing this "pedaling" as you paddle will add power to the stroke.

Next, experiment with different variations of the forward stroke, such as:
- place the paddle in very close to the kayak in an almost vertical position and pull parallel to the boat's centerline. This is your most powerful stroke — it propels the kayak the most and turns it the least. It's even more powerful if your hands are spread wider than normal. This **power stroke** is very useful for

accelerating quickly, going fast, and is essential should you need to "save your bacon" on a river when you need to quickly avoid or move through a tricky situation.

- keeping the paddle at a low angle, place it far away from the kayak as you paddle — it will fairly quickly turn the boat. Sweeping the paddle in a large arc (called a **sweep stroke**) will turn the kayak even more.
- notice that the harder you pull/push on the paddle, the more effect the stroke has.
- notice how the easiest and most comfortable forward stroke is in between the power stroke and the sweep stroke. This is the stroke you will use most often.

Get to know the difference between all of these trying out various positions of where you place the paddle by the boat and how hard you move the paddle.

Stopping

Begin by just going straight, alternating easy left and right strokes. Now imagine you need to stop in a hurry. Do this by paddling backwards with a few quick, short, but decisive strokes alternating on each side. Did it work? Great!

Now try this — move forward as fast as you can, then stop quickly. Practice this until you get good at it.

Like brakes on a car, this quick type of **back stroke** will be very useful in many situations. It is an essential "tool" to have in one's skill set.

Backing Up

Once you get a good feel for how stopping works, try moving backwards at a steady pace. This full **back stroke** is the same as going forward, but done with steady, easy backward strokes on both sides. Rotate your upper body to one side and plant the blade in the water just behind you.

Push forward parallel to the keel of the kayak as you unwind your torso. Once the blade is past your hips, lift it out the water. (Why? Because if you paddle forward of your hips the boat will start to turn.) Continue twisting your upper body until it's fully rotated to the other side and you are ready to paddle on that side. Looking behind you as you twist will help in the torso rotation as well as allow you to see if "the coast is clear".

Practice this enough so you can easily go backward in a relatively straight line. Glance behind you often to watch where you are going.

Now go forward. Stop. Go backwards. Stop. Repeat.

Being familiar with how to stop and go backwards is extremely important. Doing so will save you from hitting something (or someone) or avoid a path you do not wish to take. In fact, one of the unique aspects of kayaking is this easy ability to stop and go backwards.

On a river, paddling in reverse allows you to hold your position relative to the shore. In fact, doing so at an slight angle will allow you to **ferry** sideways across the current while pointed mostly downstream. And if the current is gentle enough, with a little more effort, paddling backwards can even move you slowly upstream.

Just as was done with the forward stroke you can "pedal" your legs on the foot rests for more power.

<u>Turning</u>

Going forward and backward is great, but just as important, maybe more so, is knowing how to turn your kayak. To do so, start by paddling on just one side for a few strokes. Notice what happens. Then reach out a little further than normal a few times. Now try sweeping the paddle around in a large arcing stroke. Notice how the more you reach out the more the boat turns, and how hard you paddle naturally affects how quickly it happens.

Remember that for the most effect, rotate your upper body as you make the stroke. If you are twisting a lot and making a large arc (called a **sweep stroke**), you are actually doing a **bow pry** at the beginning of the stroke and a **stern draw** at the end.

Practice paddling in circles, both to the left for a while, then to the right. Get comfortable with this.

Now reverse the process, paddling backwards in a large sweeping motion (called a **reverse sweep**). You'll go backward and change direction at the same time. It's a useful and "powerful" stroke. If you are twisting your upper body a lot and making a large arc, you are actually doing a **stern pry** at the beginning of the stroke and a **bow draw** at the end. Practice this. Then do this stroke alternating from one side to the other making a large "snake-like" pattern in the water with your kayak.

If you have a sit-inside kayak with thigh braces, try leaning it in the direction of your turn and notice how the boat turns even easier. Get comfortable holding an edge — that is, **edging** or maintaining a leaning boat position. It's your hips that do the leaning while your upper body and head stay upright and centered over the boat. Even without thigh braces a bit of leaning will help in making turns.

Experiment with variations on these strokes. Reach out farther or reach out less. Paddle harder or paddle easier. Use just the first half or second half of the stroke. And so on. Notice where you have more or less of an effect on the kayak's direction. Notice how a backward stroke turns you quickly but slows you down, unlike a forward stroke which does not slow you down but does not turn you as much.

Next, from a stopped position, paddle forward on one side and then backwards on the other side. What happens? You begin to spin in place! (You won't do that easily in a canoe.) The more you sweep out away from the boat, the more you'll turn. Try spinning all the way around. Then, stop yourself and spin in the other direction. Practice and get comfortable with this. This maneuver shows just how much control you have over the direction of your kayak. (Canoeists are often surprised at just how maneuverable a kayak really is compared to a canoe.)

Steering

As you are moving along, such as on a river, you can turn and do course corrections using forward or backward strokes as already covered. But you can also do so using your paddle as a rudder.

Go forward at a steady pace. Once up to speed, with your paddle's blade behind you at one side and turned vertical, put it in the water near your kayak and push out, away from the boat (called a **stern pry**). Notice how quickly you turn. Now put the paddle in the water away from your kayak and pull it towards the boat (called a **stern draw**) and see how you turn the other way. Notice how the pry stroke is the more effective of the two. You're using the paddle essentially as a rudder, turning the kayak without slowing it down very much and with little effort. These **stern rudder strokes** are very handy when guiding yourself down a river (as well as running with following seas or riding the front of a wave). You can also do pries and draws at the bow, but they are not as effective. (Though they can be very useful for the front person in a canoe or two-person kayak.)

You now know how to go forward, stop, go backwards, and turn in several different ways. Good job!

Stability

As you do all of these strokes and move around, with your feet on the foot rests and your thighs placed in the thigh braces (if you have them), rock your hips from left to right to see how stable your kayak is. Get a feel for this. How far does the boat lean before it begins to take on water? Notice how much or how little control you have over the leaning of the kayak. Those of you with thigh braces will have a lot, those without will have much less.

More Strokes and Tips

> **RECOMMENDATION**: When paddling, keep your elbows relatively low and close, and your hands typically at shoulder height or lower. Doing so will help a lot to protect your shoulder joints, as water can have a huge force on the paddle blade and therefore on you. This is especially true for whitewater and sea kayakers but is something about which all kayakers should be aware.

Pay close attention to the paddling techniques of better, more experienced paddlers and copy them. You do not want to develop bad habits now that will be difficult to break later.

See the "TAKE A PADDLING CLASS" section to learn about courses available at which you can develop the best habits now as you are learning to paddle.

A few "more advanced" strokes that you may want to explore and learn at some point are covered in the Glossary — see **brace, ferrying,** and **sculling**.

Practice Sessions

Consider some fun practice sessions with your paddling buddies to learn, teach, and/or reinforce the basic kayaking strokes and maneuvers. A few minutes of these sessions would be a good warm-up before a long trip, for example. Ideally, set up a little course with milk jug buoys and practice going through it both forwards and backwards. If any in your group knows them well include some advanced strokes, too.

If you want to take these sessions a bit further and have a very calm, warm-water lake (or similar) available, as a group practice **wet exits**, paddling swamped kayaks, towing kayaks, guiding swimmers to shore, and emptying swamped boats. It's a lot of fun and very instructive.

TESTING YOUR KAYAK

> **RECOMMENDATION**: Before you take it out on a real trip, test any "new to you" kayak to learn about its handling characteristics. With a sit-inside kayak also test filling it, swamping it with water, then emptying it. With any kayak, test tipping it all the way over.

Back in the "Test Before You Buy" section it was recommended to test your kayak before buying it. Hopefully you did that. Even if you did, it's recommended to test it out further, getting used to it so you are familiar with how it handles during the many aspects of a real trip. By practicing now, ahead of time, you will be ready for these types of challenges when they arise.

If you are new to paddling, first see the previous "EXPLORING THE BASICS" section to learn launching and landing tips as well as basic strokes and maneuvers.

On a nice day, find some calm, clean, warm, and shallow (three to four feet deep) water in which to experiment. Grab a friend and put on your swimsuits.

Basic Tests

Experiment with your seat and feet position, the foot rests (if so equipped), getting in and out, launching, and landing. On the water, test the kayak's stability and its ability to accelerate, turn, go straight, stop, spin in place, and back up. Get a good feel for the boat all around.

Lean Tests

With a **sit-on-top kayak** practice leaning the boat to see if that's even possible. Can you hold that lean (called **edging**) while maintaining your balance? It's likely you cannot without **knee straps**.

With a **sit-inside kayak**, if you have a spray skirt put that on, then practice leaning your boat over as much as 30 degrees to see what that's like. Try to hold that edge while maintaining your balance. Can you do this while paddling? Practice this on both sides.

Next, if you have a spray skirt, with a friend's help, hold yourself in a deep lean putting the edge of the cockpit in the water to make sure the spray skirt seals well and keeps water out. It's no good if it does not! Test it by leaning to both sides.

Taking on Water Tests

If you have a sit-inside kayak, do the lean tests again but this time leave the spray skirt off if you were using one. Lean the boat significantly and see what it's like as it takes on a little water. As you take in more water, notice how much lower you are in the water. Paddle around a little and notice the difference from normal. Notice how the water sloshes around and how the weight of it affects the boat's handling.

Next, perhaps with a friend's help, lean the kayak over some more and let it fill with water. Notice how very low you are in the water. Paddle around a bit and notice how difficult and unstable it is. Get familiar with this for a little while in preparation for an actual event. Remember, you may need to paddle to shore like this under difficult circumstances (winds, waves, river current, cold water) someday.

Wearing a spray skirt and avoiding situations where you are likely to take on water are two ways to mitigate this. Nonetheless, you should not be afraid to take on water and now you are familiar with doing so and accustomed as to what to expect.

Wet Exit Test

Now for perhaps the most important test — practice a "wet exit" — tipping your kayak over completely and falling out of it. You'll want your life jacket on for this if it's not on already.

Sit-on-top kayak:

Do this test in water two to three feet deep. There's not much to it — tip the boat completely over to see what that's like, falling off of it while holding on to your paddle. Then flip the kayak right-side-up and get back on while it's out in the water, such as "plopping" in seat-first from the side.

> **Note:** It's relatively easy to get back on in very shallow water. But on a real trip you'll likely be in deeper water. If you are close to shore (as any savvy recreational kayaker should be), swim to shallow water while pushing/pulling your kayak. Do so while holding onto your paddle or hook it onto the boat. But if you are far from the shore, too far to swim (beyond what any recreational kayaker should ever be), that will require a **self-rescue** or rescue with the help of those with you. See the "PERFORMING AN OPEN-WATER RESCUE" section.

Sit-inside kayak:

If you have a spray skirt, put that on before you put on your life jacket.

Before doing this test in the water, if you are wearing a spray skirt and/or have full-scale thigh braces, first practice this on dry land — removing the spray skirt and pushing yourself out of the kayak. This practice will make the actual event go smoother.

Paddle out to waist-deep water. Have a friend standing nearby as you learn this process.

Tip the boat completely over to see what that's like, falling out of it.

If you have a spray skirt on and it did not come off the kayak already, run a hand forward along the edge of the cockpit coaming to the **rip cord** (quick-release loop). Pull the cord *forward* first, then *away* from the kayak — down in this case — to get the skirt free of the coaming.

If you have decent thigh braces, relax any pressure on the foot rests and those braces then lean forward and push on the boat at your hips to easily slip out.

Do all of this while holding on to your paddle in one hand, if you can.

You'll also get to test out how well your life jacket works. ☺

If you have all the proper floats and/or bulkheads in place, your kayak should float but be very hard to push or pull as it's filled with several hundred pounds of water.

Note: For a 12-foot kayak with bulkheads, the total cockpit volume is perhaps 10 cubic feet. Water weighs 62.4 pounds per cubic foot, so if that boat's cockpit is filled with water that water weighs 624 pounds!

Roll your boat on its side to see if that empties some of the water. Please note that it's possible this will actually allow more water to enter the cockpit. See how that works for your particular kayak.

Tuck your paddle under an arm or hook onto your boat, then try swimming while pushing or pulling the swamped kayak with you. It's not easy, is it?! Now imagine being out in the deeper water of a lake, bay, or river in such a situation! It's easy to see why, to recover, you'll need to be close to shore and require help from others.

With your friend take the water-logged kayak to shore to practice emptying it. Start by slowly rolling the boat on its side, then upside down to get most of the water out. Next, lift one end, then the other, eventually rocking it back and forth and from side to side. Knowing how to effectively empty a swamped boat is invaluable "out in the field".

Do not skip this wet exit test. Having knowledge of this experience will make all the difference when you unexpectedly capsize on an actual trip. It should dispel fear and build confidence so you will not be afraid of this situation but instead be comfortable with it, because now you know just what to expect and how to handle it.

Test Your "New" Paddle

If you've just acquired a new or different paddle, check out how it works by testing it with several types of strokes. Notice how it handles for gentle strokes, power strokes, easy and hard turns, when leaning, stopping, backing up, spinning in place, and anything else you can think of.

Other Tests

Part of the testing process should include determining how you will stow any gear you are likely to take, making sure it will stay dry and well secured — so it cannot float away in the event of a capsize.

Determine which shoes work well or not with your kayak.

Now you should be reasonably familiar with your boat and paddle, how they handle, and be ready to "hit the water" on an actual paddling trip.

Play Around / Experiment

> **RECOMMENDATION**: After you've done basic testing of your kayak and before going on any substantial trip, take some to time to just play around, experiment, doing some fun and even silly things with it. Get to know your boat well and what's it like in many unusual situations, at the same time lessening fear and learning a lot.

How do we increase the enjoyment of any activity? Dispel fears and build confidence. And those are done by gaining knowledge and acquiring experience. Via this book we hope to impart some basic knowledge and required understanding. Via the recommended activities and your own trips you will gain experience.

Let's look at three main kayaking-related fears — taking on water (sit-inside kayak), tipping over, and what to do after that. To work through these, let's practice doing just that.

Begin by repeating the "Taking on Water Test" and "Wet Exit Test" covered earlier in this section, then go further. Once you have tipped over, are free of your boat, and in the water, try these...

- See what happens as you try to push/pull the kayak around. Which way works best?
- If it's is upside down, can you flip it back over?
- If it's a sit-inside, does doing so empty out any water or just add more?
- Can you climb partially onto the kayak in some way and remain afloat? (This is something you might need to do in cold water while waiting for a rescue.)
- Can you easily secure the paddle on/in the boat?
- Can you grab the stern end of the kayak and push it while kicking with your feet?
- Can you **scooch** up onto the stern and kick with your feet?
- Can you swim alongside the kayak while pulling it with one hand using the front grab loop?

Try different things, play around, and experiment. See what works well and what does not. This will be invaluable when needing to get to shore after a capsize. With play comes experience and knowledge that will be useful for all future paddling.

Another basic fear involves hitting obstacles. Doing so can lead to taking on water (sit-inside kayak) and completely tipping over. To experiment doing this is difficult to simulate in a practice environment. It would be ideal if an obstacle course with rocks and logs could be set up in calm water. Most likely this will need to be done "out in the field". So under very safe conditions practice the following:

- Scooching over mostly-submerged logs and smooth rocks.
- Encountering a mostly-submerged log or rock under the left or right side of your kayak causing it to lean severally to the opposite side.
- Hitting sideways a log that's perpendicular to the current.
- Getting stuck on a log or rock — first with little or no current, then with a steady mild one.

To learn what to do in these situations, see the "Recommendations When You Are In Trouble" in the "PADDLING RIVERS" section.

The experience you gain from experimenting with these situations will be a huge advantage when you encounter the same circumstances under normal and more difficult conditions on real trips.

PREPARING BEFORE A TRIP

Here is a quick checklist to be used just before any significant trip. Be sure you have:

- become familiar w/ all of this book's recommendations,
- dressed properly following **CARDINAL RULE III**,
- reviewed the "OTHER GEAR" section to make sure you have all you need and that it's stowed properly,
- a set of dry clothes in a dry bag,
- food and drink,
- your spray skirt if you use one,
- your life jacket,
- your paddle,
- all kayak floatation in place (and fully inflated if that applies),
- and made sure any hatch covers and the drain plug (if present) are securely in place.

WARMING UP BEFORE A TRIP

If you are about to embark on a trip of any consequence it's a good idea to do a few minutes of light activity (a very short walk or run) just before the trip, then some good overall stretching before getting in your kayak.

Once on the water, continue the warm-up by practicing all the basic maneuvers — going forward, stopping, turning, and backing up. Backing up is especially good as it helps strengthen the muscles in the front of your shoulders. Don't worry about the muscles in the back of your shoulders as they will get plenty of exercise while paddling forward during the trip.

Occasionally during the trip do some backing up for a few minutes, as well, to rest the muscles in the back of your shoulders and exercise those in front.

PADDLING LAKES (Or Similar Water)

Now it's time to explore some real water...

Lakes, in our case, include "flatwater" — close-to-shore on larger bodies of water that are very calm with little or no waves and ideally good protection from the wind — and smaller lakes (perhaps 40 acres or less) that are relatively unexposed to wind. (Note that kayaking in **tidal currents** and tidal zones is not covered.)

Calm lakes sheltered from the wind and similar types of non-flowing bodies of water are wonderful for recreational kayakers and a great place to learn. Unlike rivers there's no moving water. With calm winds any waves are minimal so it's here new kayakers feel the most comfortable. Although you have to do all the work, as there's no current to help pull you along (or push you around), you are in complete control of the forward movement of your vessel. Rarely are any bursts of energy needed; instead, paddling is a steady series of easy strokes. It's in these type of lakes that I've introduced many beginners to kayaking, from 6 to 76 years old!

Because there's no current on a lake as there is in a river, they tend to be regarded as safer and are sometimes taken for granted. In general, small, calm lakes are safer than rivers. But, one can make mistakes and conditions can change — especially on larger and/or more exposed lakes. They can be quite a force to be reckoned with for the unsavvy paddler.

Recommendations Before a Lake Trip

Perhaps the most common mistake recreational kayakers make on a lake and similar bodies of water is going too far from an accessible shore, thus unknowingly putting themselves in a situation from which they cannot easily recover. (Remember **CARDINAL RULE I**, I hope?)

To prevent that and other mistakes, the following are highly recommended before paddling on any lake:

- Follow the "CARDINAL KAYAKING RULES" and "GENERAL KAYAKING RECOMMENDATIONS" already covered.

- Be familiar with the water you are about to paddle. Be sure you know the deep and shallow areas and the presence of any shoals. Talk to others who have recently paddled this body of water.

- Consider paddling just smaller lakes, perhaps those 40 acres or less, so should you capsize, you can always easily swim to shore while pushing/pulling your kayak.

- If you do paddle a larger lake, make sure it's a very calm day, it's going to stay calm while you are out on it, and that you stay close to an accessible shore, perhaps within 200 feet. (That's not a magic number, just a rough guess of the distance one can easily swim in an emergency.)

- Do not paddle on a lake whose water temperature you are not prepared for being in for any length of time.

- Do not paddle on the lake if it's windy or likely to be very windy. Learn the prevailing winds for the lake involved before going out on it.

- Avoid paddling if there are anything other than very small waves.

- Learn about boat traffic on the lake, where it's likely to be, where the marinas and launch ramps are, etc.

- Always paddle with at least one other experienced paddler.

- If the trip is a long one and/or involves a lot of people, everyone going should review the "Responsibilities of Each Member of the Group" in the upcoming "PADDLING RIVERS" section as some of those items will apply to your lake trip.

- If need be mark the **take-out point** in some way, such as a flag, colored cloth, or similar. If the take-out is the same location as the **put-in point**, mark it before you leave. If the take-out is a location other than the put-in point, mark it before the trip when you **shuttle** vehicles. Make sure all people on the trip know what to look for at the take-out point.

- Review "The Take-out Point" section in "PADDLING RIVERS" as much of that can apply to a lake trip.

- If your plans to paddle a lake involves a take-out point that's different than the put-in point, and at the end of the trip if you or someone in your group cannot easily walk back to the put-in point, you will need to take at least two vehicles and do some shuttling before and after the trip. See the "SHUTTLING VEHICLES" section later in this book for details on how to handle that.

- Follow all of the "Recommendations for Paddling Lakes" in the next section.

Recommendations for Paddling Lakes

The following are highly recommended while paddling on a lake:

- Stay within a safe distance from shore unless you are fully skilled in **self-rescue** and the other paddlers with you are skilled in **open-water rescue**. This is likely not true for most recreational kayakers.

- Keep a reasonable distance between boats — do not crowd other kayaks nor get too far apart. Keep within sight of each other and try to not go beyond an audible distance of most, if not all, people in the group.

- Do not hesitate to call out for help or use your whistle if you are in trouble. It's better to have a false alarm than no one there to help.

- Be respectful of fishing folk on the water and give them plenty of space.

- Watch for other boaters, especially water skiers. Sometimes the one driving is not watching in front of his/her boat as required but focused on the skier. (There is *supposed to be* a "spotter" — a second person watching the skier but that's not always the case.) Be sure to not put yourself in their obvious path.
- Watch for the wake from passing motorboats, jet-skis, even huge ships. Their wake can travel a long distance. Wakes from ships and the like can quickly slam you into **rip rap** or structures at the shore as well as bounce off of those structures.
- Always approach any wake or wave perfectly perpendicular to it, in line with its direction, bow first.
- Keep aware of landmarks along the way. This is important for identifying your location on the return trip (if you are coming back this way), and/or to pinpoint your location should anything serious happen.
- Follow the "Recommendations Regarding Winds" and "Recommendations Regarding Waves" in the next two sections.

Recommendations Regarding Winds

On most lakes and/or more exposed water, there's always the issue of wind:

- Wind can slow you down, blow you off course, and stir up waves. All of these can be hazardous for recreational kayakers.
- It's recommended that you know well the area you are going to paddle as well as the prevailing, current, and expected wind direction. Plan your trip so that you are protected from the wind, such as paddling along and close by the sheltered or **offshore** side of a lake. This is even better, of course, if that shore includes hills, trees, or even tall shrubbery that will block the wind to some extent.

- If there is any wind, be aware of its direction so if it's more than just mild, you can ideally paddle with it (a **tailwind** coming from directly behind you) or if you have to, directly into it (a **headwind**). This may make your trip a bit longer but you'll have an easier time than paddling with a crosswind.

- Try to avoid paddling if there's more than just a mild **crosswind** because any amount of wind crossing you will try to turn your kayak, often into the wind — called **weathercocking** or else downwind — called **leecocking**. It can be annoying and rather challenging to handle crosswinds by having to paddle continually on one side for a long period of time.

- Paddling at a right angle to the wind is perhaps the most dangerous as it can create waves parallel to your boat which can flip it over quickly. Even without any waves, the wind at this angle, if strong enough, will try to blow you over.

- Paddling with the wind off your **rear quarter** is sort of spooky. The wind (and the waves it creates) can easily turn your kayak sideways to the direction of the wind (and the waves), maybe before you even realize what's happening.

- Paddling with the wind off your **front quarter** is the easiest type of crosswind to handle as it does not try to turn you as much, and any waves it creates you can see coming.

- Paddling directly into a 20 mph headwind will likely keep you from moving forward at all, even if you're paddling will all your effort. Expect a 10 mph headwind to cut your speed in half when paddling with your full force.

Recommendations Regarding Waves

With wind comes waves which are usually a rather "tricky business". The following will help with waves away from the shore:

- Waves can slow you down, lift your kayak, try to turn it sideways, and flip you over. All of these are hazardous for recreational kayakers.

- The best approach for paddling into an oncoming wave is perfectly perpendicular to it, for then you will see it coming and are the least likely to flip. As the wave passes under you, maintain your balance as well as direction so you stay perfectly in line with its direction.

- If the waves are coming from directly behind you, they are a little spooky as they lift your kayak from the rear. You are not too likely to flip, though, unless surprised and thrown off balance, or turned from being perfectly in line with their direction. Maintain your balance and direction as the waves pass under you.

- If your approach to a wave is at any other angle, that is, not inline with its direction, it will both lift your boat and attempt to turn it sideways making you quite vulnerable to being flipped over. Especially tricky are waves coming from a rear quarter that you may not see in time to properly respond.

- For sure if you are parallel (sideways) to a wave, perpendicular to its direction, it will flip you over very quickly, in a split-second. Never knowingly travel parallel to waves but instead stay as close as possible at a right angle to them, in line with their direction of travel.

- Having to paddle directly into or with waves may force you to deviate from heading straight towards your desired destination but you'll have a much easier time maintaining your course than traveling at any other angle to them. You will also likely be in line with the direction of the wind, which is helpful because it's not a crosswind.

- Whatever angle your boat is to the waves, as they pass under you do not stop paddling — you are more stable when your paddle is moving through the water.

The Biggest Danger

The biggest concern with lakes is if one does not follow all of the previous "Recommendations Before a Lake Trip" and "Recommendations for Paddling Lakes".

On the water, very likely the biggest danger is if one has capsized (see the following "PERFORMING A WET EXIT" section) and now needs to swim to shore while dragging one's boat and paddle. And if it's a sit-inside kayak it's likely very full of water.

Most recreational kayakers have not been trained on how to perform any sort of **open-water rescue** (see the upcoming "PERFORMING AN OPEN-WATER RESCUE" section), either via a **self-rescue** or by another trained kayaker. And if it's a sit-inside kayak, they likely do not have spray skirts and proper "sea-worthy" kayaks set up with bow and stern **bulkheads** or full **floatation**. Which is why it is imperative that they avoid getting into any situation where an open-water rescue is needed (following CARDINAL RULE I and IV.)

So, for recreational kayakers, it's best if another kayaker can just help the person in the water (**swimmer**) get to shore as soon as possible. Others in the group take care of rescuing the swimmer's boat and paddle. See "When rescuers arrive" in the upcoming "PERFORMING AN OPEN-WATER RESCUE" section.

> **RECOMMENDATION**: When paddling lakes, please be sure to follow all of the Recommendations Before A Lake Trip and Recommendations for Paddling Lakes. Doing so will make for a much safer and enjoyable trip.

A Final Note

At the end of the trip when everyone is together, take some time to talk about each person's experience. What was fun, challenging, or exciting? What was learned? What do folks look forward to doing again? And, when and where's the next trip...?!

PERFORMING A WET EXIT

A "wet exit" is leaving one's boat via the water, that is, when it's upside down, or almost. Although we all do what we can to avoid them, wet exits happen.

If you capsize with any sit-on-top kayak or in a "typical" recreational sit-inside kayak (with no spray skirt, no thigh braces, and a medium to large cockpit)— there's no issue, you will simply fall out.

If you have a sit-inside kayak and are wearing a spray skirt but have no (or minimal) thigh braces and you capsize, the weight of your body will likely pull the skirt off the boat and you will simply fall out, as well. If not, see step 2 below.

If you have a sit-inside kayak with full-scale thigh braces that you hook your legs under (see **Photo 1** in the "Kayak Thigh Braces" section) you will need to do the following:

1. Hold on to your paddle with one hand.
2. If needed, give the skirt a little help to remove it. Run a hand forward along the edge of the cockpit coaming, grab the skirt's rip cord, then pull it *forward* first then *away* (down in this case) from the kayak.
3. Lean forward, relax any pressure on the foot rests and thigh braces, and with both hands near your hips, push yourself out of the cockpit.

Once you are out of your kayak and have surfaced, grab it so it does not float away. See the following "PERFORMING AN OPEN-WATER RESCUE" section for what to do next.

With a sit-inside kayak it's highly recommended you practice a wet exit so you know what to do without much thought during a real event and are not afraid of it — see "Wet Exit Test" in the "TESTING YOUR KAYAK" section.

PERFORMING AN OPEN-WATER RESCUE

In the event that you have capsized on open water and have done a **wet exit** (see the previous section), there are several methods of self-rescue or being rescued by another kayaker. Those techniques require instruction and skills beyond the scope of this book. One self-rescue technique, once called the "Eskimo" roll, also requires a kayak that can accommodate a complete roll, being able to go from upside down to right-side up, which most recreational kayaks cannot.

The need for such a rescue implies that you are out in deep, open water, too far from shore to wade or easily swim to it. Recreational kayakers should never put themselves in that position in the first place (**CARDINAL RULE IV**). Unless you and your group are skilled in open-water rescue procedures, please do not violate that rule — stay close to shore.

Touring and sea kayakers MUST absolutely learn rescue techniques, as they will often be out in open water, more exposed to wind and waves where the likelihood of tipping over is much greater and getting to shore is much less. By the way, taking a sea kayaking course is highly recommended for any recreational kayaker who expects to paddle any type of open and/or exposed water away from shore. See the "TAKE A PADDLING CLASS" section.

Nonetheless, for the recreational paddler, if you DO capsize in open water and have performed a wet exit:

- Immediately shout out for help and/or blow your whistle.

- If your group understands **paddle signals** and you are able, use the HELP signal as well.

- Hang on to your paddle. Tucking it under an arm is one possibility.

- Stay with and hang on to your boat. Assuming it has the proper **floatation**, it will float even if filled with water. Also, a kayak is much easier for rescuers and other boaters to see than a person floating in the water, especially in waves.

- If you have separated from your kayak, while holding onto your paddle swim to the boat. Know that the wind blowing on a kayak may move it faster than you can swim to it.

- If you are being pushed into any kind of dangerous objects in the water (rocks, other boats, etc.) or at the shore (docks, piers, rocks, riprap, breaking waves, seawall, etc.), stay "upstream" of your kayak so it does not get slammed into you when you encounter the objects and potentially pin you against them. Your boat may also provide some protection when you meet up with those objects.

- If no rescuers are immediately on their way and assuming you are able, hook your paddle on/in your boat, then drag or push the kayak while swimming to the nearest accessible shore. If your boat has all the proper floatation, it will be very heavy but it should float, even if filled with water. One technique is to grab on to the back of the kayak, even scooch up on it a little for some extra floatation for yourself, then kick with your feet while pushing the boat. Once you get to knee-deep water, walk your kayak to shore.

When rescuers arrive...

- Let them know how they can help, such as rescuing you, your kayak, your paddle, and/or other loose stuff.

- Sit-inside kayaks: It will help a lot if you and your rescuer can empty as much water as possible out of your boat. Even if you have bow and stern bulkheads (or the equivalent floatation), a cockpit full of water weighs a lot (perhaps 600 pounds for a 12-foot kayak). A lighter kayak is much easier to tow. This process usually involves putting the bow of your boat across the cockpit of the rescue boat, and then you and the rescuer slowly roll your kayak over, letting water drain out. If you happen to get it nearly empty, you and the rescuer can then try "teeter-tottering" your kayak while it's upside down, rocking it from one end and one side to the other to get even more water out.

- Rescuers should follow "Bringing in an empty kayak" in the "Recommendations When Someone Else Is In Trouble" section in "PADDLING RIVERS".

- If you need to be towed in the water by another kayaker, know how to hold on to the stern grab-loop of the rescuer's boat without tipping it over. (If the rescuer goes in the water, you're both in trouble.) If you can, try to swim along, kicking your legs to minimize the drag on the rescuer. If you are not panicking you can even try to scooch up a bit onto the stern of the rescuer's kayak if he/she lets you and if you can do so without any chance of tipping the rescuer over.

- Your rescuers should follow "Helping someone ashore" in the "Recommendations When Someone Else Is In Trouble" section in "PADDLING RIVERS".

- Never put the rescuer in danger. Should that happen, he/she can no longer help you!

- Once on shore get into dry clothes as soon as possible to reduce the chance of **hypothermia**.

PADDLING RIVERS

> **RECOMMENDATION**: Rivers are a lot fun under the proper conditions. But due to the inherent danger of a the moving water involved there are myriad Do's and Don'ts for paddling a river. Please study this entire section thoroughly before venturing out on any river.

Compared to lakes, rivers are a whole other "breed of cat". The obvious difference is that they involve continually flowing water. You don't have to do as much work to move forward as on a lake, but there's a bit of a loss of control as the current wants to carry you here and there which sometimes spooks beginners. Unlike a lake, there are times where a short burst of energy is absolutely essential to avoid or recover from a tricky or potentially dangerous situation.

I think rivers are more fun once one learns how to handle them properly. They are "nature's highways" that guide you along sometimes with little or no effort. But rivers require more understanding and respect than a lake, or at least a different type of respect. The moving water of a river can be incredibly dangerous under the "wrong" conditions. The current of even a slow-moving, shallow river can have tremendous force.

Because of the dynamics of rivers and their inherent dangers, there are many mistakes recreational kayakers can make thus unknowingly putting themselves in a situation from which they cannot easily recover. What follows next are several sections with a great many recommendations and responsibilities of things to know, do, and not do, These should minimize the likelihood of any bad situation from occurring therefore making a much safer and more enjoyable trip.

By the way, the rivers this book covers are those for recreational kayaking — **Class A** through **Class II**. (See the Glossary for a full description of river classes.) "Recreational rivers" do not include any significant whitewater nor do they involve being far from shore or in remote locations from which it would be difficult to walk out or seek help.

River Dynamics

That water is moving! Do nothing and you are moving too! For those new to paddling rivers it's important to learn their basic behavior and start out on those that are easy, slow, and relatively shallow.

In the following five sub-sections, we look at the features of river dynamics and how to handle them. They are easier to see and more difficult to deal with in faster water yet are present in all rivers. The choices available to handle these features are limited in narrow rivers; more options and path choices are available with wider rivers.

It will become very clear why learning to **read the river** is so important — this is covered in detail in the upcoming "Boat Scouting" section.

Moving Across the Current

Here's an fundamental river paddling rule that's important to understand and follow when paddling in any **current**. An object floating in a current will move in the direction of that current and at the same speed, regardless of the orientation of the object. Likewise, even if your kayak is aimed in a given direction, that does not move the boat in that direction. (It will just keep moving in the direction of the current.) To actually move in a direction other than that of the current you need to **move faster than the current**. This requires giving yourself some forward momentum. The more you have the easier it is to go where you desire across the current, such as to avoid an obstacle. Obviously, the faster the current the harder you'll need to paddle to accomplish this.

The Main Current

In the **main current** or "channel" of a river the water is moving the fastest, at "full speed" for the current (pardon the pun) conditions of that river. Outside of the main current and very often along the banks on a straight section the current will likely be slower. On some gentle rivers there may be little or no current next to the banks.

On a straight section of the river the main current often runs down the center. But because of islands, rocks, tree-fall, shoals, bars, the shape of the river bottom, etc., the main current may be at one side or the other and can weave from side to side. Think of the main current like a narrow river within the actual river. The main current can sometimes be spotted by a string of bubbles traveling along with a faster current moving within the river. In the main current the water runs deeper and faster; out of it the water is shallower and slower.

If you want to slow down (or speed up), slip out of (or into) the main current. On shallow rivers, outside of the main current may be too shallow to travel. Conversely, if you are hitting the bottom, getting stuck, and are not in the main current, getting yourself in that "channel" will usually allow you to start moving again.

Generally, you want to follow the main current. But there are times when you *cannot*, such as when there are obstacles and **strainers** in the channel of the main current. And there are times when you *should* not, such as when the main current wants to pull you to the outside of a turn where obstacles are present, along a dangerous river bank, and/or where there are **sweepers** just above the water.

Where rivers widen out they usually also become slower and shallower, making following the main current even more of a necessity to avoid running aground. Conversely, where rivers narrow expect the current to be faster and the water deeper.

Obstacles in the River

They may exist, but rarely have I seen a river that did not have at least some form of **obstacle** and often more than one type. These include **tree-fall**, logs, stumps and branches, rocks, boulders, and shoals.

Rivers with a history of human use can have man-made obstacles as well, both current or remnants from some form of previous activity, perhaps just above or just below the surface. These might be dams, bridges, pilings, fences, and other structures.

Some obstacles will be exposed but many more will be submerged sometimes "lurking" just below the surface. Most obstacles cause some form of disturbance in the water. Look for any kind of upstream **pillow** or downstream foamy "bump", little wave, or other indication on the surface of the water.

But, obstacles can be deceiving. There can be hardly any pillow at all from a large rock or other obstacle just below the surface, or there can be a significant downstream bump from an obstacle that's safely a few feet below. The exact position, depth, size, and shape of the obstacle is often hard to tell from the size of the pillow or downstream bump. If possible, it's best to steer well clear of any pillow or bump. Then as you pass by, take a close look to see what's causing it and the form of the result on the water. You may be surprised at how deep or shallow an obstacle really is.

Shoals and the like can sometimes be easy to spot based on the water actively above them, such as many small **riffles**. But, those can be deceptive as well. Shoals can be made from several types of material such as sand, gravel, mud, and even dense water foliage. Watch the main current — it will usually go around any shoals. Pay close attention to the boaters ahead of you to see who makes it through, who does not, and where that occurs, especially if their kayak sits lower in the water than yours.

If the river you are paddling travels through any woods, expect trees, logs, stumps, and branches in the river, both submerged and showing as well as falling from the banks. These may combine into larger piles of "timber" and create a **strainer** (explained in a moment).

One nice aspect of kayaks over canoes is that if you get loosely stuck on certain types of obstacles, such as a mostly-submerged log or smooth rock, you can more easily **scooch** over it. (We've even scooched over very low beaver dams!)

Another form of obstacle that often "snares" novice paddlers are called **sweepers** — low-hanging branches over the river that can "sweep" you from your boat or tip you over. They can be anywhere along wooded rivers. Sweepers are common and more dangerous at the outside of turns, as the current is usually stronger there and it wants to pull you to the outside and into any obstacles or sweepers lurking there. That stronger current also erodes the river bank, so along wooded banks it's continually creating new sweepers, making any existing sweepers more prominent, and potentially turning them into strainers.

Perhaps the most dangerous type of obstacle is one that can "trap" paddlers. Called a **strainer**, it's a type of obstruction that lets water pass through but not boats and people. A collection of fallen trees and log jams are great examples. A tight grouping of boulders, patches of larger shrubbery growing in the river, and even a wire fence in the water can be strainers. They are often along riverbanks, but can be right in center and in the main current. In a turn they often on the outside. A strainer is particularly dangerous if it's in the main current, for then that current will try to carry your kayak directly into it. The current's force can easily pin your boat against a strainer. Therefore a fundamental river paddling rule is **avoid any strainer if at all possible**. Be very vigilant about watching for such obstacles and **maneuver yourself well in advance to avoid them**.

Oh how nice it would be to not have to worry about obstacles. But one should never expect that to be the case. As a river paddler you must learn to **read the river**, watch for any obstacles, and know how to avoid them. You want to continually look ahead watching for all that's coming (called **boat scouting**) so that **well in advance of any obstacle you can position your kayak to avoid it**.

That is another fundamental rule for paddling any river (or any body of water with a current) — set your course in advance of what's coming. This is essential, for if you do nothing, the current may draw you directly into an obstacle. Instead, move across the current enough so you are not in line with being pulled to that obstacle. Do not wait until you are upon it, for then it's far too late to try to avoid it due to the moving current. The longer you wait, the harder it is to get out of the way. The faster the current the quicker you will have to react to avoid the obstacle. As you go by it, while maintaining a safe distance take a close look to see what it actually is — e.g. a simple branch or a whole submerged tree?! Is it a small rock or a huge boulder lying much deeper than expected?!

Before approaching any kind of obstacle or obstruction, if you have any doubt as to what a safe path would be, immediately begin back paddling to slow down or stop, then move to the shore and wait for advice from other paddlers. If it's large enough you all may have to climb over it. If it's serious obstruction your group may need to **portage** via the shore to go around it. (Report the impediment to others who might paddle this section of river.)

<u>Turns and Bends in the River</u>

Now you know about handling the current and avoiding obstacles. Great. Well done. Now for the "interesting" part — where the river bends and turns.

The main current usually goes along the outside of a turn as shown in **Drawing C**. In that "channel" the current is the strongest and fastest, and often the river is the deepest, as shown in **Drawing D**.

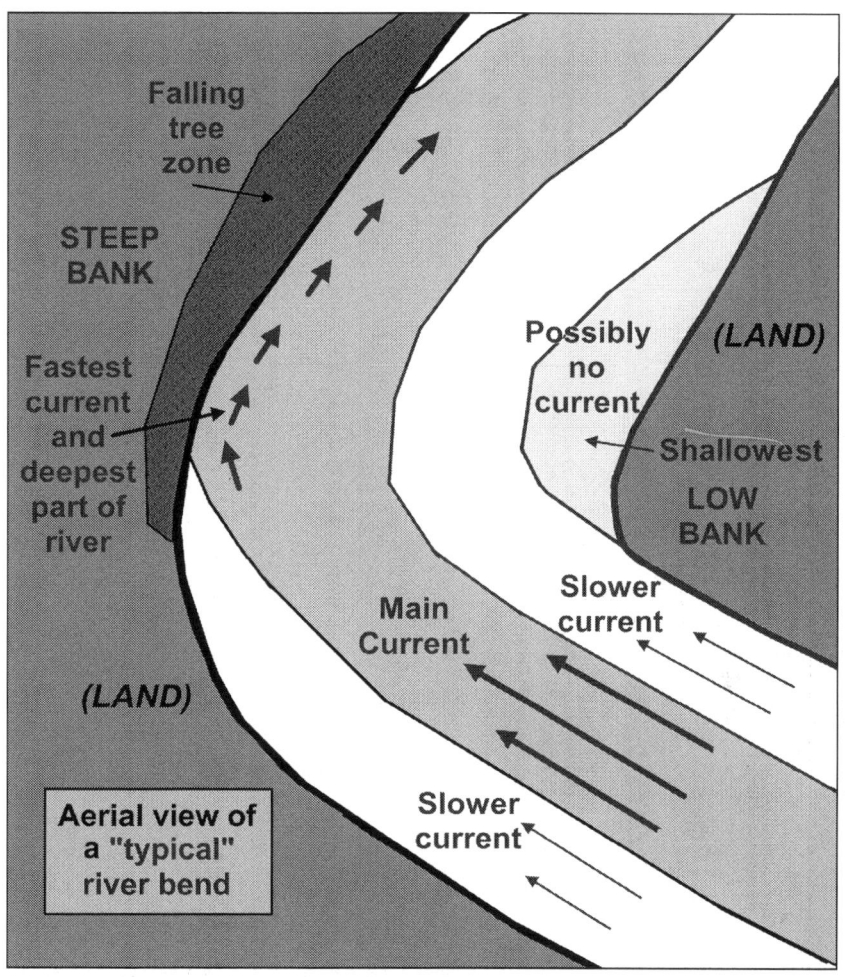

Drawing C — Aerial view of a typical river bend

The outside bank is typically much steeper than the inside bank. In a wooded area it may include overhanging sweepers and trees in the process of becoming sweepers. The strong current along the outside erodes the river bank, which brings down rocks and trees from above, potentially creating sweepers and/or strainers. Floating tree-fall and other debris often gets swept into and trapped against the outside of a turn and may pile up in that deeper water.

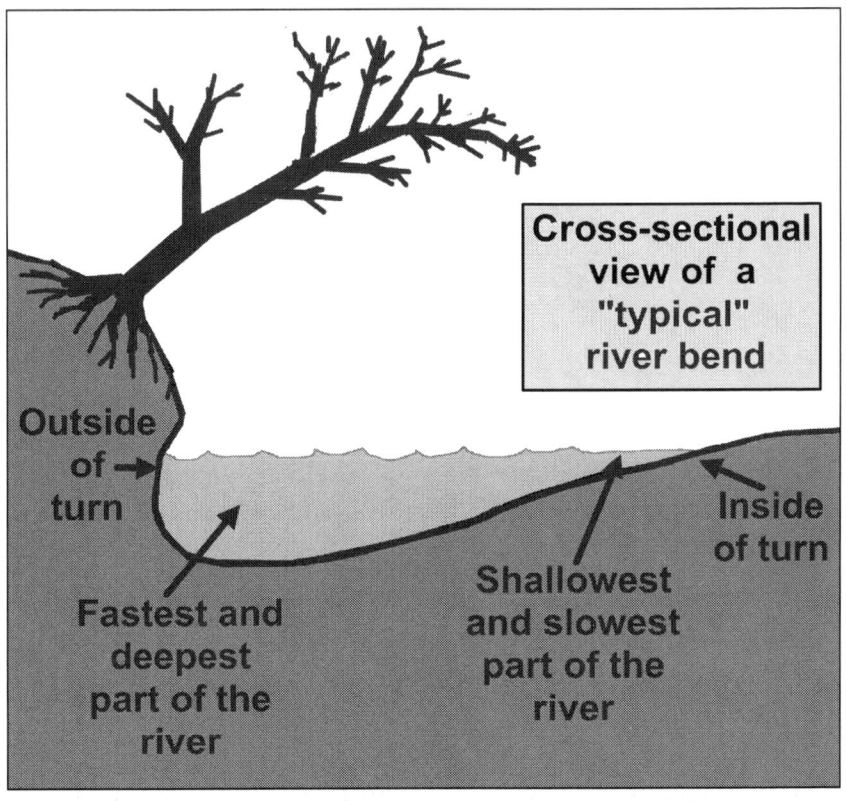

Drawing D — Cross-sectional view of a typical river bend

In a turn, if you are in the main current, it will want to take you with it to the outside of the turn and whatever lurks there. A very swift current can sometimes even pin one's boat to the outside bank.

Unless it's clearly free of obstacles and sweepers, **the outside edge of a turn should be avoided.** It's an easy and very dangerous spot to tip over! Obviously, if the river is very gentle the danger is much smaller. Just be cautious at the outside of any turn. The sharper the turn and/or the faster the current, the worse the danger can be.

On the other hand, on the inside of a turn the current will usually be the slowest and typically the river becomes much shallower as shown in **Drawing D**. It can be an easy spot to have one's bow get grabbed by very slow "inside-turn" water, then be pulled into even shallower water, potentially get spun around, and possibly run aground. I would not call it hazardous, just a disappointment, as now you've lost all forward momentum and have a little bit of work to do to get out of that situation and moving again. And those who were following too closely may be surprised and bump into you.

Typically the safest place to travel in a turn is a "happy medium" between the inside and outside of a turn. This is perhaps a third of the way away from the inside river bank. You are likely to be a bit to the inside of the main current, in between the fastest and the slowest water of the turn. That's okay, as this keeps you from getting snagged by the slowest and shallowest water on the inside, yet keeps you away from the fastest water of the main current and being pulled into the possible dangers at the outside of the turn. If you find yourself being pulled to the outside and you don't want to be, quickly move closer to the inside of the turn. Remember that you can always slow down, **back ferry**, even back up, if need be.

Just as you did with obstacles, be sure to continually scout ahead at turns in the river so you can anticipate what's coming and prepare for it. **Maneuver yourself in place well in advance of the turn.** Do not wait until you are right upon it, for then, due to the moving current it's much too late to properly position yourself and chose a safe path.

Obstacles in Turns in the River

Now you're familiar with handling the current and turns, and avoiding obstacles in straight-aways. But what if there is an obstacle in a turn, especially in your desired path?! You will have to handle the turn AND avoid the obstacle. This requires a very sharp eye to detect these situations well in advance so that you can **determine a safe path and maneuver yourself in place well before of the turn.**

You may have to go into the slower water on the inside of the turn (much safer). Or, go into the main current temporarily (not as safe) then do some quick maneuvering back out of the main current once past the obstacle. With that latter approach, because you are in the faster main current in the turn, you are much more likely to get swept to the outside bank and into any obstacles or sweepers residing there. So, the better choice is usually to take the inside of a turn to avoid the obstacle.

Often things are not so simple but involve a combination of issues, such as multiple obstacles requiring several smaller (yet potentially sharp) turns by you within the river bend. And making such maneuvers while being very aware of what the current is doing at all times.

Before entering any situation, if you have any doubt as to what a safe path would be, immediately begin back paddling to slow down or stop, then move to the shore and wait for advice from more experienced paddlers.

Boat Scouting

The act of continually looking ahead so you can anticipate what's coming and prepare a safe route through any obstacles or rapids is sometimes called "boat scouting" — scouting ahead from your boat. On recreational kayak type rivers this should be all that's required. One can also scout from the riverbank which is often needed on more difficult rivers.

When scouting, practice **reading the river**, asking questions such as:
- Where is the main current and where is it going?
- If I do nothing, where will the current take me?
- What's the least I need to do to maintain a safe path?

- What is the river doing 50, 100, and 150 feet away? Don't look at just what's right in front of you but quite a ways downstream as well so you can plan for what's coming.
- Is the water ahead moving fast or slow?
- Is that water smooth or "bumpy"?
- What's underneath all those bumps? Is it a shallow patch, or stones, rocks, branches, or other debris in deeper water?
- Are there any strong **eddy** currents (those that move much slower than, or in the opposite direction of, the main current)?
- What are the upcoming features, such as obstacles, obstructions, sweepers, strainers, rapids, islands, and shoals?
- What is the easiest path I need to take to successfully get through all of those features?
- If my first path choice does not work what are my second and third choices?
- Do I need to alert others behind me as to what's coming?
- Is it lunch time yet? ☺

Scouting is also important because depending on the situation and speed of the river, you may not have the luxury of being able to back up and go a different way. You may have just one chance to choose a safe path.

On the other hand, on rivers not very fast, if you do not like your "current" approach to a situation, you can likely do several things for a better approach, such as: slow down, stop, **ferry** (or **back ferry**) to a different side of the river, paddle backwards, or even turn around and paddle upstream. This needs to be taught to beginners and perhaps reminded to intermediate paddlers. You do not always have to follow your present path but can likely readjust for a better one.

Recommendations Before a River Trip

The following are highly recommended before paddling any river:

- Follow the "CARDINAL KAYAKING RULES" and "GENERAL KAYAKING RECOMMENDATIONS" already covered.

- **Always paddle with at least one other person and never paddle any river alone** (following CARDINAL RULE II). Period. Do people do it? Sometimes. Is it wise? Absolutely not. If anything adverse happens, of which there are many possibilities, no one is there to help. Even if you were able to call out for help, people heard you, and happen to find you, by the time they'd reach you it likely would be too late to do any good.

- **Never paddle an unknown section of river.** Before doing any section unknown to you, do all you can to learn about it from other paddlers, river guides, outfitters, comments online, local guide books, etc. Ideally paddle it with someone familiar with it.

- **Talk to others** who have (hopefully recently) paddled the section river on which you are about to travel to know its current condition and if there are any new obstacles or other issues.

- As you learn to paddle rivers better, it's fun to have others along that are similar in level to yourself so you can **learn together**. It also helps a lot to have at least a few paddlers along that are more experienced so you can **learn from them**.

- Know the **trip plan**: the exact put-in and take-out points, start and end times, specific paddle route, scheduled stops long the way, people on the trip, etc.

- Know the details of the river you are to do — its depth, speed, **gradient, classification**. Are there any narrow channels or extra-sharp turns? Is the river joined by other tributaries that dramatically change its volume and speed? Is there a lot of tree-fall? Are there any significant rapids or obstacles?

- Be sure you are able to handle the current conditions and any known challenges of the river, and be ready to learn "on the job." Also know that just because you've done one easy Class II rapids on an otherwise much easier river does not qualify you to paddle an overall Class II river.

- Know that rivers change — from year to year, season to season, even within a few days or hours (after severe weather, for example). Common short-term changes are rises or falls in the water level (and the accompanying change in speed) and new tree-fall. Therefore, always know beforehand the difficulty and current conditions of the section of the river you about to paddle.

- Know the primary compass direction of the section of river you are going to paddle and the expected wind speed and direction for when you will be paddling. You do not want a strong **headwind** most of the trip! Rivers in a valley and/or surrounded by trees will experience less wind than those in flat, open areas, but any wind present will be "channeled" by the valley and trees — so a tailwind or headwind will be more likely than a crosswind.

- Know how to spot if the river is in a high-water or flooding condition. Besides water that's much higher and/or faster than usual some of the tell-tale signs include:
    - unusually muddy, sandy, silty, or discolored water,
    - water above its normal banks possibly flowing through riverside foliage and trees in areas that are typically dry, and
    - a lot of branches, logs, trees and/or other loose debris being carried in the water.

    Avoid paddling rivers under these conditions. There are way too many additional hazards during high-water times.

- Know how to spot if the river is in a low-water condition. Besides water that's much lower and/or slower than usual some of the signs include:
    - water below its normal banks,
    - exposed river bottom at the banks,
    - shallow islands and/or exposed shoals, bars, and river bottom not normally seen, and
    - an unusual amount of **riffles**.

    You may want to avoid paddling such a river unless there's an easily-found, sufficiently-deep main current. And if not, if you do not mind getting stuck a lot, doing the "**knuckle walk**", and pulling your boat through sections too shallow to paddle.

- Be aware of any *known* obstacles, obstructions, or portages on the river and be prepared for any *unexpected* ones.

- Know all the bridges involved or at least the major ones.

- If there are any **culvert** type river crossings, before the trip verify that the culverts are completely clear, both inside as well as several feet before and after them. If not, make sure there is a way to portage around them.

- On any river likely to have tree-fall, bring at least one bow-saw along. Know where and when it's wise to cut and when it's not. Sometimes trimming a few small branches can make a difference between getting through or not. We've avoided several "messy" portages with about ten minutes of work trimming a narrow path through tree-fall that spanned the width of the river. Know that you are also helping fellow paddlers (and yourself) for future trips.

- Follow the "Recommendations for Paddling Rivers" in the next section.

Recommendations for Paddling Rivers

The following are highly recommended while paddling on a river, beginning with a few essentials learned in the previous "River Dynamics" and "Boat Scouting" sections. The first six items below are considered *fundamental river paddling rules.*

- **Scout the river** ahead of you from your kayak and if needed, from along the riverbank ahead of time. "If in doubt, get out and scout!" before doing any challenging section.

- **Read the river** continually as you paddle.

- **Well in advance** of any obstacle, turn, or other concern, determine a safe path and maneuver yourself into place to follow that path.

- To move in a direction other than that of the current you need to **move faster than the current**.

- If at all possible **avoid hitting anything** with your kayak **sideways** to the current. If you do you are extremely vulnerable to the current, being thrown off balance, taking on water, and completely tipping over.

  Therefore, **avoid being sideways** for very long as that's when you are the most vulnerable should you encounter an obstacle. Even if floating on a tame river, should you happen across a submerged stump, for example (which might have no tell-tale sign on the surface of the water), that stump could easily throw you off balance and cause you to tip over.

  In fact, when possible **keep your kayak pointed downstream**. You are in the most control this way, in the best position to maneuver where you need to go, and the least vulnerable if you encounter an obstacle.

- If at all possible avoid any **strainers**.

- Always look through any culverts (and bridges) before entering (going under) them to make sure it's clear all the way through and well past them.

- Stay within sight of those immediately in front of and behind you.

- On narrower rivers, especially those with a lot of obstacles, it's best to go through single-file. If the river is wide enough to accommodate two or more kayaks side-by-side, stay at least a boat-length or two apart to allow each person room to maneuver as needed.

- Keep a decent interval between kayaks, especially in any narrow or tricky areas, to allow each person more than enough room to navigate through without being struck by a boat from behind.

- Stay aware of others immediately in front of you. The kayak just ahead may all of a sudden get stuck, need to stop, or even back up. They have the right-of-way — give them space. Do all you can to not hit that boat. If need be, stop, even back up if you can. Alert others behind you — call out "stopping!" or "backing up!" — so they know what you are doing and can "put on the brakes" as well.

- Do not hit another kayak — unless the conditions are safe and the other person is completely in favor of it (perhaps in fun). Doing so throws the target boat off balance as well as off course, keeping it from going as intended and potentially pushing it into something its paddler was trying to avoid.

- Know how to stop quickly. This is easily done with some quick back strokes by your hip. This is a very handy way to stop, hold yourself in place, avoid a tricky spot, or keep from hitting a boat in front of you that's hung up.

- Know how to back up your kayak quickly. This is done with several decisive back strokes. Sometimes this is the only way out of a tricky situation. Just back up and try a different approach.

- Watch as others navigate through challenging sections to see what works or what does not. Give them plenty of room. If you are following them be ready to go a different way in case their path does not work.

- Do not proceed through a particularly challenging river passage if there is any chance a kayaker ahead of you may get hung up. Go through one at a time, holding back and making sure they get through okay before proceeding. Stop others coming from upstream. Use the STOP **paddle signal** if needed.

- After you go through a tricky section stop just below it, if possible, to let others coming from upstream know anything helpful. Also, watch to see that they make it through okay, and if not, see if you can lend a hand.

- Recognize and learn from someone who consistently has a better approach to paddling difficult situations. Also, try to help and advise those that consistently have a poor approach if they are open to it.

- Be open to advice and learning "new tricks" from those more experienced.

- Do not grab on to any branches, foliage, or **sweepers** overhead when trying to avoid them. If you do, you can very quickly be drawn out of your boat, take on water, and flip over. This is especially true if your kayak is sideways to the current — that's usually a guaranteed flip!

- If you need to duck to avoid things overhead, lean forward or backward but not to the left or right as it's too easy to tip over that way.

- In areas where trees, branches, and foliage are in, near, or above the water, be aware of your paddle's top, out-of-water blade so it does not encounter any of those and knock you off balance.

- Be prepared to unexpectedly hit submerged obstacles (rocks, logs, etc.) lurking just a few inches below the surface. These can knock you off balance, sometimes quickly enough to tip your boat quite a lot. If you can react fast enough you can prevent a tip-over with some quick bracing (along with a hip snap for sit-inside kayaks with thigh braces).

   This is a common way to take a "drink in the water", especially if the obstacle catches you off guard and you are moving swiftly. Sometimes an obstacle cannot be seen ahead of time because it has no tell-tale sign on the surface of the water. Such hazards can catch beginners and experts alike, the difference being how one handles the situation and how quickly. This is also why it's important to keep your kayak oriented straight ahead so if you hit an obstacle ideally you can remain pointed downstream then just push or scooch off of it.

- A common mistake a beginner can make is to be traveling very near the bank and not watching well enough ahead, then be surprised by a tree or log in the water sticking out perpendicular to the shore. If caught in this position, now you have to react very quickly to move out of the way or risk being turned sideways to the current, hitting the tree, and losing your balance. The current can then grab the upstream edge of your kayak, tip you over, and capsize your boat. If the current is strong and flows under the tree, it can take your kayak UNDER the tree. You might get pulled out of your boat, or, worse, be drawn under the tree, too. You could even become pinned between your kayak and the tree. This reinforces why it's essential to boat scout and **way upstream maneuver out of line with any upcoming obstacle** and maintain a good distance from it.

   A case in point: Many, many years ago while paddling with friends on a tame, shallow, and wide river, we happen to witness a young couple in canoe, new to paddling, who had been traveling very close to a river bank, all of a sudden be surprised by a tree sticking directly out from the shore. In an attempt to avoid it they immediately turned sideways to the tree yet hit it with the bottom of their boat as they were leaning upstream. Upon impact they lost their balance which caused the boat to tip even further upstream, just enough for the current to easily grab the gunwale of the canoe and put it underwater. As that happened the two people and their loose contents were quickly separated from the canoe. Then the boat and its remaining contents were pulled with great force under the tree. Luckily, the canoe went completely under the tree and reemerged. But it could have easily have become pinned against part of the tree underwater, held in place there by the current, and then be extremely difficult to recover.

It's a blessing the couple was able to get out in time. Had the boat become pinned they could have been trapped between it and the tree. But all their loose, non-floating contents was pulled into the water, under the tree, and much of it was lost. (I think we did help them find their cooler, at least.) Although this was in a canoe, the same thing can happen in a kayak or any boat on a river.

That one experience taught all of us many lessons about river paddling.

- Study the current and learn why it moves the way it does in any particular situation. This will help with your ability to **boat scout** and **read the river.**
- "Beware the frothy whitewater" they say. You'll see this on faster rivers. It's a very likely sign of an obstacle below — though it's depth, shape, and size are often hard to tell.
- "Head for the vee" my uncle would say. In this case he meant the "V" pointing downstream made by waves

coming from two nearby obstacles across from each other forming a large upside down V. This is generally a good idea, but certainly not always, especially when there are multiple obstacles or when the converging waves are big enough that where they meet creates significant and turbulent whitewater. (And there's the possibility that other obstacles reside under that turbulence.)

- Avoid any and all dams, weirs, and man-made drops, no matter how small. There are too many potential dangers with such structures. Always portage around them by moving to the side of the river well in advance of them and then carefully proceeding along the shore to the portage launch site below them.

- CAUTION: At any time, such as when coming ashore after a capsize, do not attempt to walk or wade in fast-moving river water that's knee deep or more. Instead, it's best to swim to avoid a foot getting hung up between rocks or other debris on the bottom, getting pushed off balance by the current, and potentially becoming trapped underwater.

Recommendations When You Are In Trouble

We've talked about basic river paddling, scouting, and doing all one can to prevent mishaps. Now we need to talk about what to do should you get in trouble. This usually means you are stuck in some way such as at or on an obstacle, or have capsized and are in the water.

- If you get hung up on top of an obstacle, such as a mostly-submerged rock, boulder, or log:
    - Avoid grabbing any branches from above. You can easily lose control of your kayak and the current will try to turn it sideways and flip it over very quickly.
    - Do all you can to stay pointed downstream. You do not want to turn sideways — unless you want to flip over.
    - If you are stuck on the *downstream* side of the obstacle, **scooch**, paddle, and/or push by hand on the obstacle to free yourself from it.
    - If you are stuck on the *upstream* side of the obstacle, things are much trickier:
        - If the current is gentle enough, you may be able to scooch backwards and back paddle enough to get off of it and go around it, hopefully without turning sideways. Usually this is **not** the case.
        - Is there any chance you can scooch, paddle, and/or push by hand on the obstacle to push yourself over it? This might work if the obstacle is small enough and/or not very high above the water's surface.
        - Can you perhaps very carefully push and scooch your kayak sideways off of the obstacle? (or backwards a little and then sideways?) This *may* work in very gentle current. Nonetheless, be very mindful of the current rushing around the

obstacle which will try to grab and turn your boat.

- Otherwise, do what you can to stabilize your boat, keep it pointed downstream, then call out for help, blow your whistle, and/or use the HELP paddle signal so others can come to help get you out of the situation.

(I've been caught in such as situation by becoming stuck on a log I thought would submerge when I encountered it but was proven wrong! So I never try to go over any log that I cannot easily scooch over should it not submerge.)

- If you are about to encounter any obstacle sideways to the current:
  - Before you do, **lean the kayak downstream**. The natural tendency is to lean upstream to encounter the obstacle with the bottom of one's boat. But if you do, once you hit the obstacle the current will quickly pile up, grab the upstream edge of the kayak, flip it over, and pull it underwater. You and your kayak could get pinned underwater up against the obstacle.

- If you become pinned sideways against an obstacle (called a **broach**):
  - Avoid grabbing any branches from above unless you want to leave your kayak. A boat sideways to the current can be flipped over quite quickly.
  - **Lean the kayak downstream.** To maintain your balance quickly do some bracing with your paddle. In a sit-inside kayak with thigh braces a quick snap of your hips will help. By leaning downstream you greatly reduce the chance of the current grabbing the upstream edge of your boat and flipping it over. Although held in place there against the obstacle, at least you will not tip over.

- o Call out for help and/or blow your whistle so others can help get you and your boat out of the situation.

- o You may be able to use your downstream hand to forcefully scooch laterally (perpendicular to the current) and slip around the obstacle.

- o Otherwise, until help arrives, do your best to stabilize your kayak and stay leaning downstream.

- o If trapped against a tree or log jam, to help stabilize your boat you may need to hug a thick branch or the trunk.

- o In more serious cases, you may need to pull yourself out of the kayak and up onto the tree. Keep your boat leaning downstream while doing so.

- o Always save yourself first, abandoning your kayak if necessary.

- In general, if you cannot recover from a given situation:

  - o Do not wait — call out loudly, "Help, Help!" This is extremely important so all those around you know what's happening and can come help. It's always best to be safe than sorry.

  - o If you have time blow your whistle as well to alert others that you need help.

  - o Use the HELP paddle signal if it makes sense to do so, you are able, and others with you know what it means.

- If you are tipping over and going in the water is inevitable, shout out NOW for help. This lets your rescuers know as soon as possible that you will need help.

- If you have capsized:
    - If you are not out of the kayak already, get out NOW. See the "PERFORMING A WET EXIT" section for dealing with spray skirts and thigh braces.
    - Shout out loud and clear for help and/or blow your whistle.
    - Hang on to your paddle. Tucking it under an arm is one possibility.
    - Stay with and hang on to your boat. If it has the proper **floatation** it will float. Also, a kayak is much easier for rescuers to see than a person floating in the water.
    - A water-filled kayak is extremely heavy and especially dangerous in a current. Stay upstream of your boat so you are not trapped between it and any obstacles or debris.
    - Not knowing if or when rescuers will arrive, it's most important to attempt to rescue yourself, getting to an accessible river bank as soon as possible. You do not want to stay in the river and be swept into any hazards downstream.
    - If you are relatively okay, in a good position to do so, and have separated from your kayak and paddle, attempt to rescue both of them. Then attach your paddle to the boat and drag or push it while swimming to shore. If your sit-inside kayak has all the proper floatation it will be very heavy but should float, even if filled with water. One technique is to grab onto the stern of the kayak, perhaps even scooch up on it a little for some extra floatation for yourself, then kick with your feet while pushing the boat. Once you get to knee-deep water and only then, walk your kayak to shore.
    - If you cannot reach your boat and the river is calm, you may be able to swim to shore. If the current is

fast and/or there are a lot of hazards it's best to float. When floating assume a *protected position*: lie on your back with your feet first pointing downstream, your toes at the water's surface, and your arms out at your sides. Use your feet to push off from any rocks or other hazards you encounter. Use your arms and strong kicks to direct yourself to shore.

- Do not stand up in the water unless it's knee-deep or less. In a fast current you can get pushed off balance and injured. If your foot becomes trapped and you get knocked over you could be held underwater.

When rescuers arrive...

- Hopefully you are with a group and others are coming from nearby to help. As they arrive let them know how they can help — rescuing you, your boat, paddle, and other loose stuff.

- If you need to be towed in the water by another kayaker, know how to hold onto the stern grab-loop of the rescuer's boat without tipping it over. (If the rescuer goes in the water you're both in trouble.) Try to swim along if you can, kicking your legs to minimize the drag on the rescuer. If you are not panicking you can even try to scooch up a bit onto the stern of the rescuer's kayak if he/she lets you and you can do so without any chance of tipping the rescuer over.

- Sometimes it's best for both parties (rescuer and rescuee) if the one in the water just swims or floats ashore on her/his own but guided by the rescuer.

- Know to never put the rescuer in danger. Should that happen, he/she can no longer help you!

- Once on land, get into dry clothes as soon as possible to reduce the chance of **hypothermia**.

Recommendations When Someone Else Is In Trouble

- If someone calls out for help and/or you recognize someone is in trouble:
    o Shout out to all upstream and downstream that the group is stopping for a rescue. Blow your whistle, if need be, to alert all within earshot. Everyone is to pass the word along to all paddlers in the group up and down the river.
    o Everyone who can should immediately go to the kayaker in trouble. If there are already a sufficient number of rescuers involved, those who are not helping directly should hang out nearby to see how they may best lend a hand, perhaps by rescuing a paddle or empty kayak.
    o If the kayak of the person in trouble is stuck on an obstacle, several paddlers need to get to him/her to see how they can help, often the most easily done by those coming from upstream of the one in trouble.
    o If the person in trouble is in the water and *upstream* of you:
        - Quickly stop and go back upstream to help.
        - The primary objective is to, as soon as possible, get to and aid the person in trouble. Do all you can to make sure at least one rescue person gets to that kayaker — typically that's someone coming from upstream of the one in trouble. Then at least one rescue person needs to help the **swimmer** ashore. See the upcoming "Helping someone ashore" subsection.
        - The secondary objective is to rescue the kayak of the person in trouble then their paddle. See the upcoming "Bringing in an empty kayak" subsection.

- Watch for any floating gear, and grab that, if possible, and/or alert and coordinate with others coming from downstream as to who can grab what.

- If the person in trouble is in the water and *downstream* of you:
    - Quickly assess how you can help, usually by getting to the kayaker in trouble as soon as possible or directing others close by to do so. Then at least one rescue person needs to help pull the **swimmer** ashore. See the upcoming "Helping someone ashore" subsection.
    - Send someone to rescue the kayak and paddle of the person in trouble, often best done by those downstream of the mishap. See the upcoming "Bringing in an empty kayak" subsection.
    - If there are enough helpers, send others after any remaining loose gear.

- Helping someone ashore:
    - For a paddler in the water (swimmer) the main thing is to get him/her to shore as soon as possible and into dry clothes.
    - You can have the swimmer hang on to the stern grab-loop of your boat. If needed, and the swimmer is able and not panicking, he/she can partially shimmy up on the stern of your kayak and grab around your waist or the cockpit coaming. But this will greatly affect the handling of your boat and make it quite unstable. In fact, no matter where the swimmer grabs your kayak, that will affect its handling and ability to turn, especially in a strong current. If the one in the water panics and pulls too hard that can even cause you to flip. You are of no help if you're in the water, too!

- Another option is to use a quick-release **tow line** that attaches around the rescuer's waist then is tossed to the swimmer. With these the tug on the rescuer is at a low point and not trying to turn or flip the rescuer's boat.
- If the swimmer is okay it may be best for both parties if the rescuer can just help the rescuee swim or float to shore.
- Make sure others in the group take care of rescuing the swimmer's kayak and paddle.
- Once on land make sure the swimmer gets into dry clothes as soon as possible to reduce the chance of **hypothermia**.

- Bringing in an empty kayak — for those rescuing the boat of the swimmer:
  - If it's a sit-inside kayak and upside down, leave it that way. It likely has air trapped inside and is therefore much lighter than if filled with water. If it's not too heavy it may be possible to tow it to shore.

    Also, if you flip the boat right-side up, doing so may fill it with a lot of water or swamp it completely. This makes it very difficult to tow. The water sloshing around inside it makes it very unstable and very heavy. Towing it can even flip a rescuer's kayak.
  - If it's sit-inside kayak that's right-side up and not filled with much water, besides towing it, a rescuer may also be able "hook" the bow of his/her kayak in the cockpit of the rescued kayak and "bulldoze" it (pushing it sideways) to shore.
  - If the kayak being rescued is a sit-inside that's right-side up and filled with water, it's difficult and dangerous to tow. Two people should push that boat ashore with their own kayaks. Like two

dolphins, one pushes near the bow and the other near the stern.

- o If the kayak being rescued is a sit-on-top that's upside down, flip it over for easy towing.
- o When towing another kayak ideally use a quick-release **tow line** attached to the rescuer's waist and the bow grab-loop of the boat being towed. Leave a good distance between kayaks so the one being towed is not constantly bumping into the rescue boat.

- Once all people and equipment are rescued and together on dry land:
  - o Leaders call for a break and make sure everyone and their equipment is accounted for.
  - o Make sure everyone who needs dry clothes or any assistance gets it.
  - o This is a great time for a group huddle. Talk about what happened, what everyone experienced, what went right, what went wrong, and how to do better next time. Thank all those that were able to help.
  - o Make sure everyone is in good physical and emotional shape then carry on with the rest of the trip.

Responsibilities of Each Member of the Group

From the two previous sections it's easy see the type of trouble one can get into and how it takes cooperation from nearly everyone in the group to help when there is such a situation. Yet with a small but vigilant effort from everyone many types of trouble can be avoided.

One should only ever paddle a river in group — two people is okay under good circumstances, a minimum of three is recommended, and five is better. But we need to define the responsibilities of everyone on the trip: the leader(s) of the group, each person in the group, specific positions within the group, and the whole group.

<u>For the leaders of a river trip:</u>

Before the trip:

- Create a **trip plan** — where and when to meet ahead of time, the exact put-in and take-out points. start and end times, specific paddle route (including through any forks and around islands), and expected stops along the way for meals and breaks.

- Make sure everyone going knows the trip plan.

- Be sure someone responsible not on the trip knows the trip plan and the names of everyone on the trip.

- Ideally, help everyone on the trip understand all the rules, recommendations, and responsibilities provided in this book for kayaking and river paddling.

- Be sure everyone knows the whistle and paddle signals you all will be using and what they mean.

- Know the exact number of people in the group.

- Meet everyone on the trip and know them all by at least their first name. Have everyone introduce themselves to each other, as well.

- Know who are the more and less experienced paddlers.

- Be aware if anyone in the group cannot swim and politely let everyone else know, as this is very important should a rescue be needed. Any non-swimmers MUST wear a full life-jacket at all times while on the water.

- Be aware if anyone has any health concerns or special needs and what's required should they need help.

- Be aware of all the bridges on the section of river you are about to paddle. Alert the group about all the bridges involved or at least the major ones.

- If any bridges are of the type likely to have obstacles or obstructions under or around them, especially culvert types, investigate them before the trip.

- Know the current condition of the section of river you are going to do and if there are any known obstacles, obstructions, or other issues.

- Make sure all people going on the trip are able to handle the current condition and challenges on the river, and if not, that they are ready and able to learn "on the job".

- Bring along any rescue and emergency equipment that might be needed. Also, review the "Gear Group Leaders Should Consider Bringing" list in the "OTHER GEAR" section.

- Make sure all drivers have their keys when they leave their cars.

- Make sure everyone in the group with a cell phone has your phone number and perhaps that of everyone else in the group.

- In some areas there may not be cell phone service. In that case, a set of waterproof "walkie-talkie" two-way radios all tuned to the same channel is invaluable. At a minimum, the **point boat**, one of the **sweep boats**, and the leader(s) should have one of these radios.

On the trip:

- Check with each paddler to see how they are doing along the trip, especially on longer ones and in the latter sections of the outing. Ask, "are you ready for a break?" If they jump at the chance, call a break for the group. It's likely other paddlers are tired and ready for a short rest as well.

- Keep an eye open for those that may be having trouble in any way, especially beginners who may be getting frustrated or those a little too quiet to complain. Anyone in discomfort could have serious issues if caught in a difficult situation.

- Watch for signs of fatigue in anyone of the group. This includes steering somewhat randomly, falling behind often when normally he/she would be up with the main group, asking repeatedly, "how much longer?", or complaining a lot about being sore. If you spot such signs, it's a good time to call for a break.

- Like a mama/papa duck take head counts of your "ducklings" regularly.

For every person on a river trip:

Before the trip:

- Make sure you know the **trip plan**. If not, see one of the leaders of the group.

- Let your leader(s) know if you cannot swim. Everyone else in the group needs to know this too, in case of a rescue. This might mean someone will need to immediately abandon their boat to save you. You MUST wear a life jacket at all times while on the water.

- Let your leader(s) know if you have any health concerns or special needs.

- Review the "Gear Each Person Should Bring" and "Gear Each Person Should Consider Bringing" lists in the

"OTHER GEAR" section to make sure you have all that's needed and desired.

- Be sure you are aware of and are able to handle the condition and challenges on the river you are about to paddle. If not, be ready and willing to learn.
- If you have a cell phone, make sure it's charged, that you have the number of the leader(s) and others in the group, and that they all have your number.
- Know the whistle and paddle signals used by the group.
- Make sure you understand all the recommendations provided in this book for kayaking and river paddling.

On the trip:

- Follow the trip plan created by the leader(s).
- Stay aware of information that's being passed "up" or "down" the line of paddlers and do your best to share it.
- If you must take an alternate route, always alert someone who is taking the main route. Make sure that other route is not off-limits according to the trip plan. Never take an alternate channel or way around an island **alone** (an aspect of **CARDINAL RULE II**).
- Be aware and keep track of all who are in front of you and behind you, whether they can be seen or not.
- If you are a more experienced paddler, stay aware of less experienced paddlers and offer tips if needed. Keep a watchful eye on them in tricky situations.
- If you are a less experienced paddler do not be afraid to seek advice from more experienced paddlers. Also, watch and learn from how they handle tricky situations.

For the point boat at the front:

Some trip organizers like to designate a specific person to be the point boat for the whole trip. Perhaps that's needed with large groups of paddlers with a mixture of experience. We've found with smaller groups, perhaps ten or less, of recreational paddlers doing just **recreational kayak water**, different people can take turns being in the lead, as desired, as long as they are aware of the responsibilities of that position.

- Follow the intended **trip plan**.
- Know when and where to stop for a meal or a break, assuming that's part of the trip plan.
- Be alert for unexpected breaks for which the leader(s) may call.
- Know how to pick a good place to stop for a meal or a break. Usually you want a place:
    - with a small, sandy, grassy, firm mud, or soft gravel beach on the edge of slow moving water so everyone can easily land and later launch;
    - with a low, relatively flat shore that's easy for everyone to get to and relax upon outside of their boats;
    - that's in or out of the sun depending on the temperature of the day;
    - that's out of the wind if it's a cool and/or windy day;
    - with areas of bushes or woods that can be used for privacy for separate his and her outdoor restrooms;
    - that offers a good swimming hole if it's a nice day and folks want to swim.
- Stop every so often to make sure all paddlers are present and okay.
- Know exactly where to stop at the **take-out** point.

- Do not go past a portage, dam, bridge, or canoe/kayak access point until you wait for the group to catch up. This helps avoid going past the take-out point accidentally. It also helps the group stay together, discuss any issues or changes, etc.

- Do not get too far ahead of the group. Keep those just behind you in sight. At the bare minimum stay within earshot of others.

- Be aware of others who go past you. (If they are a new kayaker and/or may not be aware of the point person's responsibilities, gently let them know and recommend they stay with you, or better yet, behind you.)

- Be aware of those whom you pass by and keep track of those who are immediately behind you.

- Know how to read the river well and spot any potential river hazards.

- Scout for challenging places and alert the rest of the group as needed with recommendations.

- Watch for cool stuff along the way (giant snapping turtles, etc.) and pass it on to the others.

For the second and third place positions:

- Keep track of who's in the lead.

- Stay alert for any information the point person is passing along to be shared with others upstream.

- Be aware of those immediately behind you.

- Ideally, everyone should know where everyone else is. But that only works in very small groups.

- Do not pass the point boat unless you are aware of and prepared to assume the responsibilities of that position.

For the TWO sweep boats at the rear:

Some trip organizers like to designate specific persons to be the **sweep boats** for the whole trip. Perhaps that's needed with large groups of paddlers with a mixture of experience. We've found with smaller groups, perhaps ten or less, of recreational paddlers doing just **recreational kayak water**, different people can take turns bringing up the rear, as desired, as long as they are aware of the responsibilities of that position.

- There must never be just ONE boat in the rear of the group, but always TWO, staying fairly close together, each keeping track of the other in case one gets hung up.

- Those in the last two positions have the obligation of being the "sweep boats", staying aware of other boaters ahead of them and making sure someone does not fall behind and become a SINGLE rear boat.

- Do not get too far behind the group and keep those just ahead of you in sight. At a bare minimum stay within earshot. If either of you are tired call for a break.

- Being upstream of everyone else the sweep boats are in the unique position of being able to easily get to anyone in the group should that person need assistance. (Those downstream of a person in trouble may have more of a challenge paddling upstream).

   A case in point of why TWO sweep boats are needed: Many years ago when kayaking a river with some people I did not know well, I found myself at the back of the group. That's fine, but they got far enough ahead of me that I could not see anyone nor was anyone watching for me. That seemed okay, too, unless trouble happens.

   Well, when going under a simple footbridge, I wound up hitting a submerged log and the kayak rode up onto the very pointed end of a broken branch. Once it was directly underneath me, my weight forced the boat down on the sharp branch stub, putting a hole into my plastic kayak. (They are durable but not indestructible!)

I had to get out and pull the boat off of the branch and the tree. which was not easily done as the kayak was not in a stable situation, nor was the footing very reliable.

The hole was perhaps 3/4" in diameter. I wondered how much water it will allow inside? I had no duct tape or repair kit and still had more than an hour to go before reaching my car — can I make it? Uh... no! After just a few minutes enough water came in to make the boat sit much lower in the water and very difficult to control. Those many gallons of water slowly sloshed from end to end and side to side like a "ton of bricks".

By going ashore and emptying as much water as possible I could carry on for a few more minutes, which I did a few times. Then, I'm not sure where the idea came from, but I found that one of my toes fit into the hole, enough to stop most of the water from coming in. That allowed me to finish the trip with only a couple more stops.

I was lucky for I was all alone and this was a relatively tricky river to navigate. I never saw any of the other paddlers. I wonder if any of them ever thought, "where's Jim?". And fortunately, I did not need them to shuttle my car.

A lot of lessons were learned from that one "lucky" little incident!

For the whole group:

Before the trip:

- Know how many people are in the group.

- Meet everyone on the trip, at least by first name if the group is perhaps 20 people or less. If the group is very large make sure you at least know the leaders.

- It helps if everyone knows the experience level of the other paddlers.

On the trip:

- In trickier areas it helps if a more experienced paddler goes first so those less experienced can learn and see what's best to do.

- It helps if a more experienced paddler can be one of the sweep boats at the end so he/she can help someone in trouble downstream, if needed.

- With a large group it helps to "sandwich" less experienced paddlers in between more experienced ones.

- Keep the group relatively close together. Think of it like a giant rubber band, one that can stretch out quite a ways and yet remain one whole entity, never breaking into separate groups (unless that's planned for and known in advance).

- Maintain plenty of spacing between kayaks to avoid collisions. Space yourselves close enough to permit communication but not so close as to interfere with one another in challenging spots.

- If the group is large, consider dividing into smaller groups or using the "**buddy system**" as an additional safeguard.

- Watch for the two sweep boats at the rear to make sure they are keeping up with the group.

- Watch for anyone in distress or not having a good time. Work to resolve what's troubling them.
- Know that cooperation is key!

After the trip:

- When everyone is together at the end of a trip is a great time to talk about each person's experience. What was fun, challenging, or exciting? What was learned? What do folks look forward to doing again? And, when and where's the next trip...?!

The Take-out Point

> **RECOMMENDATION**: Make sure all paddlers on a trip know the exact take-out point and do not go past it!

Sometimes things can get messed up at the **take-out** point, especially on a river, with people not stopping but going past it for various reasons. This is not a good situation. Do all you can to avoid this, including:

- If possible along the way while setting up shuttle vehicles, show all paddlers the take-out point and what it looks like. This works well if you are passing the take-out point on the way to the put-in point.

- At the take-out point if there's not a very obvious landmark such as a bridge, those who are placing a car there are to mark it with a red flag or something similar,

- Before getting on the water make sure all paddlers have a full understanding of the take-out point, what to watch for, and where exactly to exit the water.

- As paddlers finish the trip, always have a few "watchers" posted to monitor the river for those still coming to make sure those paddlers do not go past the take-out point.

However, if you go past the take-out point:

- As soon as you realize this, contact someone else in the group, ideally the leader, via cell phone or two-way radio.

- If you are not too far past the take-out point and the current allows, paddle upstream back to it.

- Only if that's not possible and hopefully the river allows (is not too challenging), paddle to the next dam, bridge, or canoe/kayak access point so you can be found by those searching for you.

- If it's not possible for some reason, stop at a place along the river where you can be seen (and ideally accessed) from a road or path that's along the river. Then those searching for you can at least see you and hopefully get to you. If you have a whistle that should help others find you.

If you are the leader and someone goes past the take-out point:

- Check with others in the group to see if the "lost" person has called via a cell phone or two-way radio.

- Keep someone posted at the take-out point in case the "lost" person happens to paddle upstream back to that point. If so, that someone is to contact the leader.

- Send someone by car to the next dam, bridge, or canoe/kayak access point to wait there for the "lost" person in case he/she goes that far. Make sure they have orders of what do to if the lost person is found, such as contact the leader.

- If need be, also send someone by car to look at every river viewing point that's before the next dam, bridge, or access point with orders of what do to if the lost person is found.

- If there's a trail along the river, this is the next best option. Send someone on the trail to look at all of the river viewing points and accessible river banks with orders of what to do if the lost person is found.

- If need be, send a small team by boat to the next dam, bridge, or access point with orders of what to do if the lost person is found.

- If none of that works, alert the local authorities.

- Be sure to coordinate all search parties by creating plans for each group — what to do if they find or do not find the person(s) lost — so in the end everyone is back together.

- Once everyone is safe, comfortable, and together again, is a good time to discuss what happened, what worked, what did not, and how everyone can do better next time. Thank all of those who helped.

Cell phones really shine in this situation. Are your phones charged? Is there service where you will be paddling? Does everyone have everyone else's phone number or at least that of the leaders? Two-way radios are the next best choice, especially if there's any chance there might not be cell phone service.

The messiness of this rescue mission reinforces the need to make sure ahead of time that everyone knows the exact take-out point, including which side of a river and bridge, if applicable, and what to watch for. Leaders — make sure everyone in your group knows this. Paddlers — be sure you know this before getting on the water.

VI. EVERYTHING ELSE

SHUTTLING VEHICLES

If your paddle trip involves ending at a location different from the starting point and at least one of the vehicle drivers cannot easily walk back from the **take-out** point to the **put-in** point, at least two vehicles will be needed and some shuttling will be required before and after the trip. This is common on river trips or any trip where there is significant distance between the put-in and take-out points.

The following methods will help with the details of shuttling everyone and everything. Feel free to make your own variations of these if needed, just be sure to work out an exact plan *before* the trip.

Note that if the trip you'd like to take is relatively far away and/or you do not have enough vehicles to do a shuttle, call a kayak/canoe livery in the area of the trip. Often for a small fee they will help shuttle your vehicle.

> **RECOMMENDATION**: Before heading out on a paddle trip, when everyone meets with vehicles and boats, work out the **shuttle plan** for before and after the trip. You do not want any surprises!

Before leaving any vehicles anywhere, always make sure that the drivers have their keys and everything needed from their vehicles. Make it your job to ask each driver, "Do you have your keys and everything needed?".

General Shuttling Method #1 — When the take-out point is NOT on the way to the put-in point:

- If it makes sense, have everyone meet at a mutually close location for all paddlers. (For those that live far away and/or closer to the **put-in** location, have them meet everyone there. If that's the case, they should jump to the "At the put-in point" step.)

- Load all boats and gear onto as few vehicles as possible making sure those vehicles can hold all the paddlers.

- *Optional:* If two or more drivers happen to be carrying an extra set of keys, consider swapping those spare sets with another driver. This is helpful if a particular vehicle is needed and its driver is unexpectedly not available.

- Drive those vehicles to the put-in point.

- At the put-in point, unload everything — people, kayaks, and gear. Make sure everyone has everything they brought along for the trip.

- Take all vehicles to the take-out point with ONLY the drivers of those vehicles. Those left behind are to keep an eye on everything.

- At the take-out point, show all drivers what it looks like so they can easily spot it at the end of the trip.
    - Before leaving, ask all drivers if they have their keys and everything needed from their vehicles.

- In as few vehicles as possible, shuttle the drivers back to the put-in point.

- Do the trip.

- At the end of the trip, in a second shuttle vehicle someone takes the driver(s) of the first shuttle vehicle(s) to the put-in point. Those left behind are to keep an eye on everything.

- Retrieve the first shuttle vehicle(s), then all shuttle vehicles return to the take-out point.

- If any drivers exchanged keys with anyone they should swap those back now.

- Load all people, kayaks, and gear.

- Go for ice cream!

- Return to the original meeting place, if needed, to pick up any vehicles left there.

At the end of the trip there are several possible variations on this. One of those is — if the second shuttle vehicle can carry all of the first shuttle vehicle's people, kayaks, and gear as well as its own, then at the end of the trip. all people, kayaks, and gear involved are loaded into the second shuttle vehicle. It then drives to the put-in point. From there, neither vehicle needs to return to the take-out point.

Another variation is — at the end of a trip, anyone not involved in any of the shuttle operations can leave, BUT ONLY IF there is at least one person left to keep an eye on the remaining boats while others shuttle vehicles.

General Shuttling Method #2 — When the take-out point IS on the way to the put-in point:

- If it makes sense, have everyone meet at a mutually close location for all paddlers. (For those that live far away and/or closer to the take-out location, have them meet everyone there. If that's the case, they should jump to the "At the take-out point" step.)

- Determine a shuttle vehicle. It will not carry any boats but be used only to shuttle drivers back to their vehicles at the end of the trip. It must hold all the drivers. (More than one shuttle vehicle may be needed.) The kayak and gear of the shuttle vehicle's driver is loaded onto another vehicle.

- Load all boats and gear onto as few vehicles as possible making sure those vehicles can hold all the paddlers.

- *Optional*: If two or more drivers happen to be carrying an extra set of keys, consider swapping those spare sets with another driver. This is helpful if a particular vehicle is needed and its driver is unexpectedly not available.

- Drive the shuttle vehicle and all vehicles with gear to the take-out point.
- At the take-out point show all paddlers what it looks like so they can easily spot it at the end of the trip.
- Leave the designated shuttle vehicle. That driver now rides in another vehicle.
    - Before leaving, ask the driver of that vehicle if he/she has his/her keys and everything needed from his/her vehicle.
- Drive all other vehicles to the put-in point.
- Unload everything — people, kayaks, and gear.
- Do the trip.
- At the end of the trip, the shuttle vehicle takes all drivers to the put-in point to get their vehicles. Non-drivers stay and keep an eye on everything.
- If any drivers exchanged keys with anyone they should swap those back now.
- All vehicles return to the take-out point. (Actually, the shuttle vehicle can now leave from the put-in point, if desired, assuming the original carrier of that vehicle's boats and gear will pick those up.)
- Load all people, kayaks, and gear.
- Go for ice cream!
- Return to the original meeting place, if needed, to pick up any vehicles left there.

Special Shuttling Case for Two Paddlers

This scenario is if there are just two people going on a trip, both have a vehicle, but only one can carry kayaks. This requires going to the take-out point before the trip and some extra shuttling after the trip — but it works:

- Meet at a mutually close location for both paddlers, such as where the boats are stored.
- Load both kayaks and gear on to the *carrying vehicle* making sure that vehicle can accommodate two paddlers. (The other vehicle is called the *shuttle vehicle*.)
- *Optional*: If both drivers happen to be carrying an extra set of keys, consider swapping those spare sets with each other. This is helpful if a particular vehicle is needed and its driver is unexpectedly not available.
- Drive both vehicles to the take-out point.
    - Before leaving, ask the driver of the shuttle vehicle if he/she has his/her keys and everything needed from his/her vehicle!!
- Leave the shuttle vehicle and take the carrying vehicle and both paddlers to the put-in point.
- Unload everything.
- Do the trip.
- At the take-out point, one person drives the shuttle vehicle to the put-in point and the other person keeps an eye on everything.
    - Before leaving, make sure the driver has the keys to the carrying vehicle.
- At the put-in point, the driver leaves the shuttle vehicle and takes the carrying vehicle back to the take-out point.
- Load all kayaks, gear, and people,
- Drive back to the put-in point.
- If you exchanged any extra keys, swap those back now.
- Each driver now drives his/her own vehicle.
- Go for ice cream!
- Return to the original meeting place.
- Unload kayaks and gear.

CARRYING YOUR KAYAK

Because you normally should never paddle alone but always with at least one other person, and since by far the easiest way to carry a kayak is with two people, one at each end, two of you should have little trouble carrying your boat to/from your vehicle to the launch site.

If you do have to carry a kayak alone:

- With lighter sit-inside kayaks, some can be carried by balancing the cockpit coaming on your shoulder. Put some form of padding on your shoulder and hang on to the coaming.

- With heavier sit-inside kayaks, you may be able to carry them a very short distance by grabbing the nearby edge of the cockpit opening with both hands. However, It's hard to walk and can be hard on your back.

- Otherwise, various forms of kayak carts (a.k.a. kayak wheels and kayak dolly) are available. These are a set of two wheels that strap onto your boat in the middle or the end allowing you to load it with all your gear and easily pull it to/from the launch site. If the cart is well-placed in the middle of the kayak, there's almost no weight on your arm as it guides the bow of the boat. Nicer kayak carts fold up and can be placed inside your kayak — then they are easily available at the end of your trip.

If you have no choice but to drag your boat, be sure to follow what has been said several times already — never, ever drag any kayak across any rough surface (such as gravel, concrete, or asphalt) but only on soft surfaces (such as sand, grass, soft dirt, or firm mud).

TRANSPORTING YOUR KAYAK

There are several ways to transport your kayak such as on top of or inside a vehicle, in the bed of a pick-up truck, or on a trailer. Determine how you will do that before you buy a boat, if possible.

More damage can be done to a kayak if it's not properly tied down while transporting it than in the water. At highway speeds and/or with high winds, kayaks catch the wind quite well and will try to lift up and/or twist off. (I see this a quite frequently when the area where I live becomes filled with many visiting kayakers).

If there's any chance of rain and your sit-inside kayak is not being transported inside a vehicle, be sure it's placed upside down or that you put on a **cockpit cover**. You do not want that water sloshing around inside the boat or the extra weight.

Choosing Tie-downs

When tying down a kayak in a truck bed, to a trailer, on a roof-top rack or foam rubber block system...

- Do not use **basic shock cords** — elastic cords made from multiple strands of rubber wrapped with cotton or polypropylene with hooks on each end. The common ones are not strong enough to do the job. They might work if they were 1/2" in diameter or more, but the common ones are typically just 1/4" to 3/8" thick and so are good only for light-duty tasks.

- You can use **rope**, for sure, if you know how to tie good knots to it them tight. The bowline, trucker's hitch, rolling hitch, and half hitch are good knots to know for this application. But ropes take longer than other methods and are more likely to stretch and work themselves loose.

- You can use solid rubber **bungee straps** IF they are in good shape, are of high-quality rubber, you do not stretch them too far, you always store them unstretched and out of the sun, and use *two* of them in the same place — to provide the proper strength and in case one breaks. (My original set of bungee straps has lasted 25 years, so far!) These are quick to put on and take off, especially if you have good connection points already established. These work best if the kayak is nicely cradled on racks in some way and not just sitting on a flat surface.

- What's best is to use **nylon straps**. These are made from strong, flat, nylon webbing. They are commonly 1" wide, are easy to put on, and do not stretch or easily wear out. The easiest ones to use have a cam buckle and hooks at each end. There are also versions with ratchets instead of buckles (often called ratchet tie-downs), just be very careful not to get those too tight. (Tip: open stretches of flat straps like these can vibrate in the wind, so put a few twists in them to lessen the vibration.)

Regardless of your tie-down system, if you are going a long distance, on a regular basis stop and check that all equipment is secure and all tie-downs are good and tight.

Transporting on Top of a Vehicle

If your kayak is going on top of a vehicle, you'll need to determine a rack system (or at least a foam rubber block and strap system). Yakima, Thule, Malone, and others make rack systems to fit a lot of vehicles. Basic rack systems are available for pick-up truck caps as well.

If the vehicle already has a roof rack you may be able customize your own kayak rack system that connects to the existing rack, such as simply attaching your own crossbars. Customize the crossbars to fit your needs. The best rack system cradles your boat nicely, conforming well to its contour.

For what it's worth: So that I can handle kayaks besides just my own, my front rack is a padded shallow "V" that fits most boats. On my rear rack I use 1/2" diameter nylon rope suspended between two short pieces of vertical 2" x 4" with notches in them to hold the rope. This accommodates any shape of kayak, right-side up or upside down. The 2" x 4" pieces fold down when not in use. (I have two such systems side by side so I can nicely carry two kayaks.)

Using racks:

If you intend to use the roof rack that came with a vehicle, check with the manufacturer to find out the weight limit of the rack to make sure it's secure enough to handle kayaks and additional racks attached to them. Some vehicle's roof racks are essentially just cosmetic.

If you are transporting your kayak on top of a vehicle using any kind of rack system, if the cradles that the kayak sits on:

- are apart a distance of at least 40% of the length of the boat (e.g. 4 feet for a 10-foot boat),
- are centered around the widest part of the kayak,
- cradle the boat tightly conforming well to its contour,

then it's likely you can get by without connections to the bow and stern of the kayak, at least for short distances at non-freeway speeds.

However, if one or more of those three things are **not** the case, you need to also connect straps or ropes (but never shock cord) from the bow and stern of the kayak to the vehicle. Be very careful not to get these connections overly tight as you can easily bend a boat too much. At both ends, it's best if you can use two lines from the kayak to the vehicle, starting at the same point (typically the grab loop) and spreading out to make an upside down "V". This keeps the end of the boat from angling sideways while traveling. Attach these to secure locations on the vehicle's bumper or frame.

When your kayak is on any type of a rack on top of a vehicle, although you have tie-downs across the middle and maybe at the bow and stern tied to the vehicle, the kayak may still be vulnerable to sliding forward in an emergency stop. This is especially true if your middle tie-downs are not very far apart, the kayak is not cradled snugly in the racks, and/or the bow or stern of the kayak is behind its connection to the vehicle. If this is true in your situation it's highly recommended to attach an **emergency stop tie-down**, such as a nylon strap or rope (but never shock cord or a bungee strap) going from the kayak's bow grab-loop to the front rack on the vehicle.

If your paddle is the two-piece kind, take it apart and secure the pieces well inside a sit-inside kayak or better yet, inside the vehicle. If the paddle is a one-piece version, ideally carry it inside the vehicle. If it will not fit, tie it to the racks or the kayak in a secure way.

Loading on racks when alone:

By far the easiest way to load a kayak onto roof racks is with two people. Since you should never paddle alone, hopefully you will have a helper.

If you are alone, have to load a kayak onto racks yourself, and it's too heavy to lift all at once, here's a technique that will work for some of you with a station wagon, van, or SUV type of vehicle that has you never lifting more than about 60% of the weight of the boat.

- Place a towel (or similar) on the rear rack or cradle if it's not a roller rack. This will allow the kayak to slide.

- Place a towel (or similar) on the back edge of the vehicle's roof in line with where the kayak will sit on the rack.

- Place a pad or towel on the ground behind the vehicle in line with where the kayak will sit and at a distance of around 75% of the length of the kayak.

- Carry the kayak to the vehicle, place its stern on the pad or towel on the ground behind the vehicle, and place the bow on the ground along the nearest side of the vehicle.

- Lift the boat's bow onto the towel on the back edge of the vehicle.

- Lift the kayak's stern and slide it forward through the rear rack and fully onto the racks or into the cradles.

- If it makes sense with your rack system and there is any chance it will rain while your sit-inside kayak is on the vehicle, flip it over so it's upside down or put on a **cockpit cover.**

- Remove the towel from the rear rack and grab the other towels or pad.

- Tie down the boat.

- To unload, reverse the process.

This process can also be used on a **basic car with a trunk**, but with one addition. Use a large bath towel and fold it length-wise in thirds. Use that towel to cover the back of the car, starting on the roof from behind the rear rack, down the back window, then over and across the back edge of the trunk, In this case, you will be sliding the kayak up onto the rear rack via that towel. The kayak will be a bit unwieldy at times, you'll have more weight to manage, and care must be taken not to drop the bow of the boat on the rear window.

The process above is certainly not the only way to load a kayak on top of a vehicle by yourself, but it is the easiest. If you go online, YouTube (for example) shows all sorts of "contraptions" designed to help one self-load a kayak. You'll find fancy and expensive systems you can buy, most of which help you load and lift the kayak onto your existing racks from the side of the vehicle. You will also see gadgets you can make that allow you to load your kayak from the side or the rear of the vehicle. Some techniques even have you strapping a kayak cart upside down on the back of the vehicle. I recommend looking for whatever is the simplest solution for your particular kayak, rack system, and vehicle. Start with the process covered above, then adapt it to your situation.

<u>Using a foam rubber block and strap system:</u>

If you do not have a roof rack or the rack that's present is insufficient to carry a kayak and are transporting just one kayak at non-freeway speeds for a short distance, then you may be able to use slightly-contoured foam rubber blocks to support the kayak and tie it to the roof of the vehicle with nylon straps. Such block and strap systems are available at paddle sports stores.

Spread the two foam blocks apart as far as possible taking into account the fact that the tie-down for each block needs to go through the OPEN front or rear doorway (NOT the windows) of the vehicle. Center the widest part of the boat between the foam blocks. You'll still need to tie down the bow and stern of the boat as covered in the previous "Using racks" subsection.

It's very likely you will also need to attach an **emergency stop tie-down** from the front grab-loop, back along the kayak, then down to the rear bumper to prevent the boat from sliding forward in an emergency stop. Use a nylon strap or rope (but never shock cord or a bungee strap).

If your paddle is the two-piece kind, take it apart and secure the pieces well inside a sit-inside kayak or better yet, inside the vehicle. If the paddle is a one-piece version, ideally carry it inside the vehicle. If it will not fit, tie it securely to the kayak.

Transporting in a Truck Bed

If you are transporting kayaks in the bed of a pick-up, be sure to tie a rope or nylon strap from the stern grab-loop of each boat to the truck. Never use shock cords. If you are carrying several boats, tie a rope or strap over the mid-section of the group of kayaks, as well, connecting both ends of it to the truck.

If your paddles are the two-piece kind, take them apart and secure them well inside a sit-inside kayak or better yet, inside the vehicle. If any of the paddles are the one-piece type and/or you are transporting no sit-inside kayak, tie them to the boats in some secure way.

Transporting on a Trailer

When transporting kayaks using racks on a trailer, what's best is to have some form of cradles that conform well to the boats, "cradling" them snugly. The cradles should be apart a distance of at least 40% of the length of the kayaks (e.g. 4 feet for a 10-foot boat). The kayaks should be placed so the cradles are centered around each boat's widest part. If all of those are true then it's likely you can get by without connections to the kayak's bow and stern, at least for short distances at non-freeway speeds.

However, if any of those things is **not** the case, then you need to also connect nylon straps or ropes (never shock cords or bungee straps) from the bow and stern of the kayaks to the trailer. Be very careful not to get these connections super tight, as you can easily bend a boat too much. Also, do what's needed to make sure the kayaks are prevented from shifting and angling on the racks at high speed and/or high winds. (This might happen if there are no cradles or "horizontal stabilizers" and the boats are just sitting on a flat crossbar.)

If your paddles are the two-piece kind, take them apart and secure them well inside a sit-inside kayak or better yet, inside the vehicle. If any of paddles are the one-piece kind and/or you are not transporting a sit-inside kayak, ideally carry them inside the vehicle. If they will not fit, tie them securely to the racks or a kayak.

Transporting Inside a Vehicle

When loading a kayak into a vehicle as well as once it's in place, do all you can to make sure the boat does not and cannot hit the vehicle's windshield. especially in an emergency stop. If you do not it's very easy to damage the windshield.

MAINTAINING YOUR KAYAK AND GEAR

On a regular basis and at least once a year, give your kayak and other gear some T.L.C. (tender loving care).

- Check for wear and tear on the hull looking for deep scrapes, gouges, cuts, thin spots, fractures, cracks, etc.

- Check the deck or top-side, as well. Inspect any hull seams.

- Inspect any bulkheads, hatch covers, deck/top-side line connection points, drain plugs, and other holes in the boat to make sure they are sealing properly.

- If you added bow or stern floats make sure they are fully inflated and secured in place.

- Check foot rests, the seat, and seat adjustments to make sure they are operating normally.

- Make sure all movable parts are in good working order.

- Make sure all parts that should be secure are fastened on tight.

- Inspect all on-board straps and deck/top-side lines for any wear.

- Check all plastic fittings to make sure they are not broken or becoming brittle.

- Add to this list anything needed for your kayak's particular features.

If any bulkhead is not sealing properly, contact the shop where you purchased the kayak or the manufacturer for the recommended sealant that will adhere well to both the bulkhead and the hull materials. Then reseal it as needed.

Inspect all parts of your paddle for their general condition. Inspect your spare paddle as well.

For a two-piece paddle, take it apart then inspect and clean the joint (**ferrule**). Make sure it comes apart and goes back together easily. If the joint allows for an adjustable feathering angle, make sure that adjustment works well.

Once a year at least, and more if used a lot, check your dry bags and dry boxes for water tightness.

Check your first aid kit and restock as needed.

Inspect any other gear you regularly take with you.

Check all your kayak rack tie-down straps and ropes for wear and tear.

Check your rack system, Lubricate any moving parts. Make sure all parts that should be secure are fastened on tight.

If you use a trailer inspect that as well.

Wash that boat and gear...

Now is a good time to clean your kayak. Be sure to remove any invasive species that might be attached to prevent spreading them to other bodies of water. Wash well around all moving parts.

If you used the boat in salt water and use roof-top racks, rinse off your vehicle as well, as the salt from that water can lead to rust and corrosion. You can clean them both at the same time by washing your kayak while it's still on the vehicle's racks. Some folks like to wash their kayaks, inside and out, after every trip.

After washing, make sure it's dry inside before putting back any hatch cover or putting on a **cockpit cover.**

Rinse all gear, such as your PFD, spray skirt, paddling jacket and pants, gloves, shoes, and paddle in fresh water after each trip, especially if they were used in salt water. (It's amazing how "unpopular" shoes that get wet from a paddle trip can smell!)

Perhaps twice a year and after washing them, apply a marine anti-UV agent to rubber hatch covers to prevent them from prematurely aging. In fact, use that same UV protectant on the entire kayak as well, especially if it sees a lot of sun.

STORING YOUR KAYAK

Before you store your kayak for a long period of time, clean it inside and out, especially if you used it in salt water. See "Wash that boat and gear" in the previous section.

For a sit-inside kayak put on a **cockpit cover**. You can buy these specific for your kayak model or easily make one with some plastic sheeting and shock cord. The cover will keep debris out of the boat as well as any type of critters that think your kayak would make a nice home.

Although you can store your boat outside in the open, such as leaning it against the side of a garage, it's recommended that you not do that. Yes, it can be stored outside, but put on a cockpit cover (sit-inside kayak), turn it upside down, and keep it off the ground. Also keep it from getting wet — this will actually keep it cleaner — such as under a tarp or small roof.

It's best to store your boat inside, if possible, such as in a garage, shed, or well-sheltered under a good roof.

Wherever you store your kayak, by all means make sure it's completely out of the sun, as "our solar provider" plays havoc with plastic and dries out rubber deck/topside lines and hatch covers.

If you set your kayak on horizontal braces, they should be padded and conform well to the shape of the boat. Or let the kayak rest upon or hang from nylon straps, so it's less likely to change shape over time, especially with plastic kayaks in warmer temperatures. For a sit-inside kayak the supports are best if they are placed where the bulkheads are, or would be if present, which is just in front of the foot rests and roughly 6" behind the back of the seat. Hang or support the boat on its edge so it's less likely to bend.

TAKE A PADDLING CLASS

It's hard to beat practical experience accompanied by professional instruction so taking some recreational kayaking classes is highly recommended. Doing so will significantly improve and enhance your kayaking skills. Check with your local paddling club, paddle-sports shop, canoe/kayak liveries, even the community college and adult education catalogs for paddling classes in your area. The American Canoe Association is also an excellent resource for paddlers and offers classes for many types of paddling. (See *www.americancanoe.org*.)

Even if you never plan to do any sea kayaking, taking a sea kayaking course is highly recommended for any recreational kayaker who expects to paddle (or be caught in) open, more exposed water away from shore. Such a course will teach you how to handle the conditions typical of that type of water and rescue yourself or others in the event of a capsize. You'll also learn techniques that will enhance your recreational kayaking skills. Anyone who kayaks with you needs to be aware of the proper rescue procedures, as well, so drag your paddling friends to the sea kayaking course, too!

JOIN A PADDLING CLUB

Consider joining a paddling club in your area. You'll meet a lot of like-minded people, learn more about kayaks and paddling, be able to test out other boats, explore other aspects of kayaking, learn about many areas to paddle, find out the conditions of local rivers, and go on trips you might not otherwise. Clubs should know about any paddling classes in the area, most of which should be beneficial. For recreational kayakers a paddling club is one of the "funnest", easiest, and least expensive ways to learn a lot.

A FEW FINAL THOUGHTS

All the do's and don'ts of kayaking are very likely overwhelming at first. But please read through them all carefully, as I believe you'll learn a lot. You'll determine those that work best for your situation, making your whole experience much safer and a lot more fun.

We've had to cover many of the potential dangers of recreational kayaking but please do not let those scare you away from this very enjoyable sport. Armed with common sense, good basic skills, the recommendations in this book, plus a little practice, you'll dispel fears, gain confidence, and be able to safely and competently experience much of what recreational kayaking has to offer. You'll soon become quite the *savvy paddler*!

Besides the type of paddling mentioned in this book, there's much more you can do with your kayak, such as fishing, camping, diving, snorkeling, surfing, touring, even sailing (with some extra attachments), Though it's true, boats more specific to those purposes certainly help.

By the way, should you want to fish from a kayak, of course you *could* buy one designed specifically for anglers with many fishing features. But you may not *need* to buy a whole new boat, because in some cases, the simple addition of just a paddle/rod holder to your existing kayak may be all that's required.

Of course, most kids and many dogs will enjoy kayaking, too. (Hint, hint!)

As you gain experience as a recreational kayaker you may find you want more and there's plenty more out there, such as whitewater, surf, sea, tandem, and race kayaking.

Through kayaking in its many forms you'll be able to explore aspects of the planet few people ever get to experience. Some of the prettiest and wildest aspects of the natural world can be accessed in no other way except via the wonderful invention of a kayak. I sincerely hope you get to experience this!

VII. GLOSSARY

Access point — any point at which you can access the water from land. This includes the **put-in** and **take-out** points and any point of access along the way during a trip.

Back face — the non-power face of a paddle's blade, also called the backside of the blade. It catches the water when you paddle backwards. (See also **power face**.)

Back ferry — see **ferrying**.

Back stroke — to paddle backwards — the opposite of a forward stroke. A back stroke is both your brakes and "reverse gear" (way to move backwards) in a kayak.

Bar — in a river, a much shallower area of elevated sediment, typically sand or gravel, deposited there by the current. In a lake or ocean, sometimes there are **sand bars** — near-shore ridges of sand typically parallel to the shore and built up by wave action. (See also **shoal**.)

Beam — the width of a boat at its widest point. It's sometimes measured at the **waterline** and if so, it will likely be slightly different than the boat's overall width.

Bilge pump — a small, hand-operated pump that's easy to carry and used to pump water out of a kayak.

Blade — the wide, thin part at the end of the paddle that goes in the water during a stroke. Blades can be long and narrow, short and wide, or somewhere in between. They can be symmetrical or asymmetrical, and they can be flat, cupped (curved along the length), or spooned-shaped (curved along the length and width).

Boat scouting — while in your boat on a river, the act of continually looking ahead, **reading the river**, anticipating what's coming, and preparing a route through any obstacles, turns, shallow areas, rapids, or other concerns.

Bow — the front of a boat. (See also **stern**.)

Bow draw stroke — see **draw stroke**.

Bow float — in a sit-inside kayak, some form of floatation in the front of the boat. The ideal bow float completely fills that end of the kayak. (See also **float bag** and **stern float**.)

Bow pry stroke — see **pry stroke**.

Brace — a supportive paddle maneuver (not really a stroke) used to regain and/or maintain your balance. Commonly used in kayaks with thigh braces by whitewater and sea kayakers along with a quick movement of their lower body. See **high brace** and **low brace**. See also **sculling brace** covered under **sculling**. (This should not be confused with **thigh braces**.)

Broach — on a river, to be pinned sideways against an obstacle and held there by the current. On a lake or ocean, to be sideways to the waves, a situation where a capsize will usually follow and is very dangerous in shallow water such as near a shore.

Buddy system — an arrangement in a group where individuals are paired together and assume responsibility for one another's welfare. This can be useful on kayak trips, especially on river trips, and for sure for the two **sweep boats** at the rear of the group.

Bulkhead — in a sit-inside kayak, a cross-sectional foam or plastic wall glued in place in front of the foot rests or behind the seat creating a watertight compartment. It provides floatation when water enters the boat by significantly lessening the amount of water that can be held inside. Bulkheads also provide some structural support. They are notorious for leaking so be sure to inspect them on a regular basis and reseal them if needed.

Bungee straps — black, flat, solid-rubber straps with metal S-hooks at each end, typically made from EDPM rubber that's UV and heat resistant. These are NOT the same as **shock cord** (a.k.a. stretch cord or bungee cord), which is used when bungee jumping.

Capsize — to completely flip a boat over. This is usually immediately followed by a **wet exit**.

Cardinal kayaker rules — rules by which all kayakers must live. To ignore these puts yourself and possibly others in great peril. These are explained in the "CARDINAL KAYAKING RULES" section.

Chart — see **nautical chart**.

Chine — the edge where the bottom of the hull meets the side. It might be a "hard" chine, which is a very sharp edge, or a "soft" chine, which is a rounded edge.

Chute — a narrower passage of river where the rate of descent and speed of the current are typically significantly greater than the surrounding sections.

Class A, B, and C rivers — non-whitewater rivers in the range for recreational kayaking. See **classification of rivers**.

Class I and II rivers — whitewater rivers in the range for recreational kayaking. See **classification of rivers**.

Class III and higher rivers — whitewater rivers beyond recreational kayaking. See **classification of rivers** for details about Class II and lower rivers, which are those in the range for recreational kayaking.

Classification of rivers — rivers are divided into nine classes: Class A, B, and C for non-whitewater, and Class I, II, III, IV, V, and VI for whitewater (according to the International Scale for River Difficulty). Recreational kayakers doing "recreational kayak water" will be doing rivers Class II and easier. In detail, those classes are:

Non-whitewater classes...
- A **Class A** river has a current of less that two knots and its motion is barely noticeable. Back-paddling is very easy.

- A **Class B** river has a current of two to four knots. Back-paddling against the current is relatively easy with some effort.
- A **Class C** river has a current of four knots or more. Paddling upstream against the current for short distances is possible but with some difficulty. Back-paddling against the current is difficult.

Whitewater classes in the range for recreational kayaking...

- A **Class I** river is considered "easy" (for whitewater kayakers) with fast-moving water without great force or volume but with riffles and small waves less than a foot in height. There are few obstacles; all are obvious and easily avoided with little training. The correct route is obvious and easy to follow. Suitable for whitewater beginners and okay for recreational kayakers. The risk to **swimmers** is slight and self-rescue is easy.
- A **Class II** river is considered "novice" (for whitewater kayakers) with a slightly faster current, straightforward rapids, and wide, clear channels which are evident without scouting from the river banks. Some narrow channels and sharp turns may be involved. Occasional maneuvering may be required, but rocks and medium-sized waves (one to two feet in height) are easily avoided by trained paddlers with reasonably quick decisions and reactions. The water may be fairly turbulent. Requires good control of one's boat and water-reading skills. At the top end of the range for recreational kayakers. Okay for whitewater kayaking beginners if they are in the presence of more experienced paddlers. **Swimmers** are seldom injured and group assistance, while helpful, is seldom needed.

Some say *real* whitewater does not start until Class III. But also, most "sane" kayakers will not paddle anything higher than Class IV. By the way, you are not likely to see real whitewater kayakers on Class I water, or lower, as that's just too easy for them (and too hard for them to go straight).

Even if you know the class for the river, it helps to know if most of the river is that particular classification or just occasional sections. Know, too, that the class of a river can change, such as during a spring flood or right after a heavy rain.

Tidbit: For those in North America, it's interesting to know that most of its rivers are no harder than Class II over most of their length. That provides a great deal of "river opportunity" besides just calm lakes and the like for the recreational kayaker.

Coaming — for a sit-inside kayak, the lip in the deck around the edge of the cockpit opening. It provides a little rigidity around that opening, keeps some of the water that's flowing across the deck from coming inside the boat, and provides a place of attachment for a **spray skirt**.

Cockpit — for a sit-inside kayak, the area within the opening in the **deck** in which one sits. The size of the cockpit that manufacturer's list is really the length and width of that opening.

Cockpit cover — a.k.a. travel cover — a cover over the cockpit opening of a sit-inside kayak made from a waterproof material. Like a **spray skirt**, make sure it seals well around the coaming. While traveling, at least, the cover should keep rain out of the cockpit. When a kayak is in storage the cover also keeps out dirt and critters.

When transporting the boat with a cover be sure to tuck the cover's release loop inside, or better yet, tie it to a deck line — otherwise the cover could come flying off at highway speeds. (You may not be as lucky as I was to have a "Good Samaritan" chase you for miles to return it!)

Crosswind — any wind not parallel to one's direction of travel. Crosswinds attempt to change the course of boats, turning them or pushing them sideways. The most troublesome crosswind is usually one that's perpendicular to one's direction of travel. Crosswinds also come from the front and rear quarters — called a **quartering wind**. (See also **headwind** and **tailwind**.)

Culvert — a plastic, metal, or concrete tube through which a creek or river passes. Typically these are embedded in soil to allow a trail, road, or railroad to cross over the water. On navigable rivers culverts are large enough to allow small boat traffic through them.

Current — on a river or stream, the downhill and mostly lateral flow of water. Its speed is influenced by the volume of water present, channel geometry, and the amount of **gradient**. For example, at any given time on relatively nearby sections of a river (therefore assuming the same volume of water), the current is faster and the depth greater in narrow sections, and the current is slower and the depth less in wider sections. (See also **tidal current**.)

> CAUTION: Be aware of rivers with large dams that occasionally release an abundance of water at one time, because the height of the river and the speed of the current can temporarily increase significantly. (The ones I know about have an alarm system downstream of the dam to warn people on the river.) Expect to see similar results after a heavy rain.

Day hatch — seen in some "fancier" sea kayaks, this is a small additional hatch near the cockpit that provides a watertight compartment that's easy to access while paddling. This hatch is isolated from the others and the cockpit so even if it floods with water that's okay as the water cannot go any further.

Deck — on a sit-inside kayak, the often-arched top half of the boat spanning its length and width (going across the **gunwales**) and enclosing the **hull**.

Deck lines — a.k.a. deck rigging — common on a sit-inside kayaks, this is nylon rope or elastic shock cord attached to the deck that allows you carry light cargo (called cargo lines), or grab onto the boat while you are in the water at points around the perimeter other than at the ends (called perimeter lines or grab lines). Deck lines should not be used to carry a kayak or for help when getting in or out. (See also **top-side rigging**.)

Downstream — on a river, the direction in which the water is flowing away from you. By the way, the *left* and *right* sides of a river refer to those sides as seen when looking downstream. You may see these referred to as **river left** and **river right**. (See also **upstream**.)

Downwind — the direction the wind is blowing; to go with the wind. (See also **upwind**.)

Draft — the vertical distance between the waterline of a boat and the bottom-most part of its keel. The draft changes with the amount of weight in the boat. For kayaks the same length, the width and **hull shape** have significant influence on the draft.

Drain plug — a small stopper device that allows one to drain water out of a kayak's hull. When present, it is usually located in the stern and can be found on both sit-inside and sit-on-top kayaks. If your boat has one, be sure to check it before every trip.

Draw stroke — a stroke made by placing the paddle away from the kayak and pulling it towards the boat.

When done at the stern, the **stern draw stroke** is a simple and effective way to the turn the kayak and best used when moving. To do this, turn the paddle's blade vertical and place it in the water behind you, a little ways away from the boat. Then, pull the blade in towards the kayak. Combined with a **stern pry stroke**, you're using the paddle as a rudder — called a **stern rudder stroke**.

There's also a **bow draw stroke** but it's not very effective (except at the end of a **reverse sweep stroke**).

And there is the basic **sideways draw stroke** done directly from the side of the boat. But it, too, is not very effective. (See also **sculling**.)

Drop — a very quick, steep descent or actual fall in a river. (It's sometimes used to refer to a river's **gradient**.)

Dry bag — a waterproof storage bag available in many sizes and colors. Bright colors are recommended so they can be seen when floating in the water. If the bag is to be stowed in a **hatch**, make sure it will fit when the bag is full. There are also clear, soft-plastic, voice-through dry bags that allow you to hear and speak through them, useful with cell phones and two-way radios.

Never trust built-in watertight kayak hatches alone to be 100% waterproof. Anything that must stay dry needs to be in a dry bag or **dry box** and also in a hatch, if possible.

Note that a basic garbage bag is NOT a good dry storage bag. A large, heavy-duty, re-sealable freezer bag will work in a pinch, or better yet, one inside another. Then go make the investment in a high-quality, durable dry bag with a good seal.

Dry box — a waterproof storage container, typically a hard plastic box with a lid that seals with a rubber **O-ring**. Anything that must stay dry needs to be in one or a **dry bag**, as well as in a hatch, if possible. (Never trust built-in watertight kayak hatches alone to be 100% waterproof.)

Eddy — on a river, the typically upstream flow of water on the downstream side of an obstacle or protruding shore, or along the inside river bank of a sharp turn. The speed and direction of the **eddy current** ranges from slower than the **main current** to moving quickly upstream in the opposite direction of that current. Eddies can be fun to play with, going into and out of them, but they can spin you around very quickly as well. Be aware of eddy currents so you can properly avoid them and/or turn into or out of them as desired.

Eddy current — the flow of water in an **eddy**.

Eddy line — the interface between the **eddy current** and the **main current** of a river. It's very important to be able to locate these for turning into or out of an **eddy** or avoiding it altogether.

Eddy turn — turning into and out of an **eddy**, sometimes called "catching an eddy" and "peeling out" respectively.

Edging — a.k.a. carving — holding an edge, that is, maintaining a leaning kayak position. This is done by tilting your hips to one side but keeping your upper body and head upright and centered over the boat. Edging is typically done when making a turn to increase its effectiveness, needed with longer kayaks.

Emergency plan — a plan made by the leaders of a paddle trip in preparation for any serious medical emergency. Explained in detail in the "GENERAL KAYAKING RECOMMENDATIONS" section.

Emergency stop tie-down — when transporting a kayak on top of a vehicle, a nylon strap or rope (never a shock cord or a bungee strap) that goes from the kayak's bow grab-loop to the front rack on the vehicle to prevent the boat from sliding forward in an emergency stop. (With a foam rubber block carrying system, the emergency stop tie-down is run from the bow grab-loop back along the kayak and down to the vehicle's rear bumper.)

Feather —

1) an offset of the angle between the two blades of a double-bladed paddle along the shaft's axis, typically 60 or 90 degrees. Sea kayakers using modern paddles typically want a feathered paddle — where the blades are not in the same plane — so the blade that's not in the water sees little resistance and slices quickly through the air.

2) to slightly rotate the paddle shaft while the paddle is in the water. This changes the angle of the blade presented to the water and is used when **sculling** and during a **stern rudder stroke** to make minor course corrections.

Ferrule — the joint or connector in the middle of a two-piece, double-bladed paddle. Typically the two pieces are held together by a spring-lock release button. Most ferrules offer an adjustment to change the **feathering** angle of the blades.

Ferrying — crossing a river laterally, moving across the current without moving downstream. Ferrying is a very valuable technique allowing you to maneuver around obstacles that otherwise might be difficult to avoid or simply move directly across a river. It's very handy to have in one's "bag of tricks".

For the standard **forward ferry**, point your boat upstream but at a slight angle towards your destination. Paddle steadily to counteract the flow of the current. You are not moving upstream or downstream but are slowly moving towards the shore and sideways to the direction of the current. The faster the current the less of an angle you can use and the more effort (and time) it will take. If you angle the kayak too much and/or you are not paddling fast enough, you will be swept downstream and likely turned around in the process.

On the other hand, if the current is gentle enough, you can ferry while staying pointed downstream but paddling backwards — called a **back ferry**. To do so, keep your boat pointing downstream but angle the stern slightly towards your destination. Paddle steadily to counteract the flow of the current. It's convenient because you do not have to take the time to turn around and you can see what lies beyond you downstream. But, it's not as effective and powerful as the forward ferry as all the strokes involved are **back strokes**.

Flatwater — very calm, unexposed water with good protection from the wind such as a sheltered bay, small sheltered lake, or very slow-moving sheltered river.

Float bag — a.k.a. bladder — in a sit-inside kayak, an inflatable waterproof bag that fills the bow or stern end of the boat. It provides floatation when water enters the kayak by displacing the water and significantly lessening the amount that can be held inside.

Be sure the float bag fills well the end of the boat — for the bow that's from just in front of the foot rests to the front point; for the stern that's from just behind the seat to the back point. Some models of float bags can be opened, re-sealed, and re-inflated and used as storage bags for cargo. These types are especially handy when **touring**.

Floatation (for kayaks) — floating material (typically foam rubber, **float bags**, or **bow** and **stern floats**) used in the ends of a sit-inside kayak to displace water and therefore provide floatation when the boat takes on water. **Bulkheads** do the same thing by creating watertight compartments that displace water that then provides floatation.

Following sea — waves or swells coming from directly behind you, heading in the same direction you are — they are "following" you and very likely passing under and by you. (See also **head sea** and **quartering sea**.)

Foot rests — a.k.a. foot braces or foot pegs — adjustable pedals (in sit-inside and some sit-on-top kayaks) or notches molded into the boat (in some sit-on-top kayaks) upon which you rest your feet. Using these, along with **thigh braces** if available, provides the paddler with much more control of the kayak and helps maintain a better posture.

Forward ferry — see **ferrying**.

Freeboard — the vertical distance from the **waterline** to the **gunwale** of the boat.

Front quarter — while traveling in a boat, the quarter-circle of horizontal area from directly in front of the boat to that directly (90 degrees) to the side. There is a left front quarter and a right front quarter. (See also **rear quarter**, **quartering sea**, and **quartering wind**.)

Gradient — the amount a river descends over a given distance, typically measured in feet per mile. Sometimes also called the river's **drop**.

- Five feet per mile is a gentle, easy gradient.
- Ten feet per mile is more "fun" and vigorous.
- A gradient of 20 feet per mile is very likely on the high end of what most recreational kayakers want to paddle.
- A steep gradient of 30 feet per mile is quite beyond what a recreational kayaker can handle and is getting into **Class III** territory (a significant whitewater river).
- A river with a gradient of 40 feet per mile very likely IS one that's Class III or beyond.

The higher the gradient, the more turbulent the river. The actual **classification of the river** depends on several other factors beyond just the gradient, such as the volume of water, speed of the current, width, depth, wave height, any rapids, and difficulty of the obstacles involved.

Even if you know the *average* gradient for a river there may be sections along the way with much lower and higher gradients (especially if a waterfall is involved!).

Grab-loop — the loop or handle at the bow and stern of a kayak used to carry it.

Gravel bar — see **bar** and also **shoal**.

Gunwale — the edge or intersection where the **deck** (sit-inside) or **top-side** (sit-on-top) meets the top of the sides of a kayak's **hull**.

Hatch — a watertight storage compartment built into a kayak. In a sit-inside kayak it is usually created by the presence of a bulkhead. Access to a hatch is via a **hatch cover**. Never trust kayak hatches alone to be 100% waterproof. Anything that must stay dry needs to be in a **dry bag** or **dry box** as well.

Hatch cover — sometimes incorrectly called a hatch — the cover of the opening in the deck or top-side to a **hatch**. Typical hatch covers are rubber, a rubber and plastic combination, all plastic, or a neoprene cap followed by a plastic cover.

Be sure to keep clean of any foreign material the area where the cover seals to the kayak, especially with rubber hatch covers. It's recommended to regularly apply an anti-UV agent to rubber hatch covers to prevent them from aging prematurely.

Head sea — waves or swells coming directly at you against your direction of travel. (See also **following sea** and **quartering sea**.)

Headwind — wind coming directly at you against your direction of travel. (See also **crosswind**, **quartering wind**, and **tailwind**.)

Heat stroke — a.k.a. sunstroke and officially known as hyperthermia — the opposite of **hypothermia** — a serious medical condition that occurs when one's body generates more heat that it can remove.

If severe enough heat stroke is life threatening. It's a very real danger when exerting oneself (such as on a long paddle trip) in direct sun on a hot day. Therefore, it's important to stay cool (wearing light-colored, loose-fitting clothing), protected from the sun, hydrated, well-fed, and not become over-tired. Avoid any alcohol. (See also **hypothermia**.)

High brace — a bracing paddle maneuver used to make major corrections to regain one's balance. The paddle is positioned perpendicular to the kayak with the power face facing the water, your elbows kept low, and your forearms angled up. On the bracing side of the boat the water is slapped hard then you pull yourself up into position to regain your balance. This is typically used in kayaks with thigh braces along with a quick snap of one's hips. (See also **brace** and **low brace**.)

Hole —

1) on a non-whitewater river, a much-deeper-than-average pocket of water often found at the outside of a turn (and typically a good place to find fish).

2) on a whitewater river, a hole or "hydraulic" is made when water pours over a submerged object causing the surface water to flow back upstream towards the object.

Hull — the bottom and sides of a kayak, below the **deck** for a sit-inside kayak and below the **top-side** for a sit-on-top.

Hull shape — the cross-section of the **hull** across the width of the boat at its widest point (**beam**). Of consideration at this point are the sides, **chines**, and bottom. See **Drawing A** in the "Kayak Hull Shape" section for common hull shapes.

Hull speed — see **maximum efficient hull speed**.

Hyperthermia — see **heat stroke**.

Hypothermia — the opposite of **heat stroke** — a serious medical condition when one's core body temperature drops significantly and the body cannot restore the heat being lost.

It's a very real danger in cold air and especially for boaters if the water temperature is less than warm and they go in. It can happen even during summer conditions to a fatigued, fully-drenched paddler.

The most important thing is to get out of the water as soon as possible, as water sucks away heat from one's body much faster than air. If severe enough hypothermia is life threatening. That's why CARDINAL RULE III is, "Always prepare and dress for going and being in the water." Even if you do not go in the water, in cool or cold air it's important to stay warm, dry, hydrated, well-fed, and not become over-tired. Avoid any alcohol. (See also **heat stroke**.)

Kayak — originally a long, narrow, single-person, enclosed watercraft propelled by a double-bladed paddle. It was developed thousands of years ago by the indigenous Aleut, Inuit, and Yupik people in sub-artic regions for hunting and fishing at sea. In fact, the word kayak means "hunter's boat".

That original idea has been taken on by many others around the world and expanded into myriad shapes and sizes for a variety of uses.

The primary concern in this book is the **recreational kayak**. We compare these often with **sea** and **whitewater kayaks**. See also **touring kayak**.

Kayak cart — a.k.a. kayak wheels and kayak dolly — a set of two wheels that strap onto the kayak in the middle or the end allowing one person to easily transport it from a vehicle to/from a launch site. Some carts fold up for easy storage inside a kayak.

Kayak touring — see **touring**.

Keel — the longitudinal centerline of the bottom of the hull of the boat, sometimes called the keel line.

Knee straps — also called leg straps or thigh straps — an accessory for sit-on-top kayaks that provides a little bit of lean control of the boat and used by squeezing one's knees together.

Knot — a measurement of speed often used in meteorology as well as maritime and air navigation.

1 knot = 1 nautical mile per hour = 1.151 mph

It came about from looking at the speed of a vessel traveling along a meridian. The vessel's speed is said to be one knot if it travels one minute of geographic latitude in one hour along a meridian.

Knuckle walk — in water not quite deep enough for your kayak to float, you can put your hands in the water, bend your fingers at the second knuckle, and while pushing up on the river/lake bottom, slightly lift and propel the boat forward while still inside it. It's not terribly effective, but it can work for very short distances and is handy if you do not feel like getting out of your kayak.

Lee side — the side of an object sheltered from the wind. (See also **windward side**.)

Leecock — the tendency of a boat to turn away from the direction the wind is from and towards that which it's blowing, that is, **downwind**. The opposite of **weathercocking**.

Length (kayak) — the overall length of a kayak. (See also **waterline length**.)

Life jacket — see PFD.

Low brace — a bracing paddle maneuver used to maintain one's balance or make minor corrections to regain it. The paddle is positioned perpendicular to the kayak with the back face of the blade facing the water, your forearms angled down, and your elbows higher than "normal" but not above the shoulders. On the bracing side of the boat the water is slapped hard then you push yourself up into position to regain your balance. This is typically used in kayaks with thigh braces along with a quick snap of one's hips. (See also **brace** and **high brace**.)

Magic Patch — an instant-setting adhesive sealant which can repair many materials. Heat the end of the Magic Patch stick for a moment with a match or lighter, then use it to repair boots, waders, tents, boats, scuba gear, leather, etc.

Main current — a.k.a. main channel — the primary current within a river where water is moving the fastest, at "full speed" for the conditions of that river, and is typically the deepest part (ignoring **holes**). It may run down the center of a straight section of a river or weave from side to side. In a turn the main current will usually be on the outside of the turn — depending on several factors such as the width, speed, and volume of the river, the shape of the river bottom, and any obstacles or obstructions involved. Outside of the main current the water moves slower and in some cases near the river banks it may not be moving at all creating an **eddy**.

Maximum efficient (or practical) hull speed — for a boat with a displacement hull (such as a kayak or canoe), the fastest that hull can go through the water regardless of the amount of effort or horsepower applied. To go faster is possible only with an extraordinary increase in power. The maximum speed in **knots** is the square root of the **waterline length** (not overall length) in feet multiplied by 1.34. A kayak with a waterline length of 8.5 feet has a maximum hull speed of 3.9 knots, and one that's 14.5 feet has a maximum speed of 5.1 knots.

That difference may not seem like a lot, but it's very noticeable when paddling. This is because a longer kayak will very likely also have a narrower and more efficient **hull shape**. So, with the increase in a kayak's length also comes an increase in *efficiency*, which means for the same amount of effort a longer boat moves easier and accelerates faster than a shorter boat. Said another way, more effort is required in a shorter kayak than a longer one to maintain a given speed.

Minicell foam — a lightweight, closed-cell (does not hold water) foam with very fine cell texture giving it a smooth, velvet-like feel and excellent cushioning properties. There are several types of minicell foam, ranging from somewhat soft to very stiff.

Minicell foam can be carved into just about any shape. Typical kayaking uses for it include seats, cockpit hip and knee padding, backrests, bulkheads, bow and stern pillars, general cushioning and padding, and car-top cradles. It's held in place with waterproof glue or contact cement, or purchased with adhesive already applied so one can just "peel and stick".

Nautical chart — A fundamental tool for the mariner, a map of a body of water showing the configuration of the shoreline and seafloor, providing water depths, locations of dangers to navigation, locations and characteristics of aids to navigation, anchorages, and many other navigational features. See *www.nauticalcharts.noaa.gov* for those charts offered by NOAA which cover U.S coastal regions, harbors, the Great Lakes, and navigable inland waters. Versions of these are also available from commercial mapmakers that provide greater detail over a smaller area and are generally easier to use.

NOAA — The National Oceanic and Atmospheric Administration — a scientific agency within the U.S. Department of Commerce that focuses on the conditions of the oceans and the atmosphere. One of their operations is the NWS — National Weather Service.

NWR — NOAA Weather Radio — from their Web site (*www.nws.noaa.gov/nwr*), "a nationwide network of radio stations broadcasting continuous weather information directly from the nearest National Weather Service office. NWR broadcasts official Weather Service warnings, watches, forecasts, and other hazard information 24 hours a day, 7 days a week. NWR requires a special radio receiver or scanner capable of picking up the signal. Broadcasts are found in the VHF public service band at these seven frequencies (MHz): 162.400, 162.425, 162.450, 162.475, 162.500, 162.525, and 162.550."

O-ring — In our case, a ring of pliable, solid rubber used in **dryboxes** and some other waterproof devices to seal out water at the interface where two halves come together.

Obstacle — any impediment to moving forward on the water. These include **tree-fall**, logs, stumps and branches, rocks, boulders, and shoals. There can be man-made obstacles as well, such as dams, bridges, pilings, fences, and other structures. These are of the greatest concern on rivers.

Obstruction — on a river, a major impediment to moving forward, usually blocking all or a significant part of the river — for example a huge fallen tree or collection of several trees across the river.

Off-stroke side — the side of the boat opposite of the one on which you are paddling. (See also **on-stroke side**.)

Offshore — (See also **onshore**.)

1) on a given shore of a body of water, that which is moving away from the shore and out to sea. "There's a strong, offshore wind today."

2) situated or occurring at sea some distance from the shore. For example an offshore oil rig.

On-stroke side — the side of the boat on which you are paddling. (See also **off-stroke side**.)

Onshore — (See also **offshore**.)

1) on a given shore of a body of water, that which is coming to the shore from out at sea. "It's a calm, onshore breeze today."

2) situated or occurring on land near the shore.

Open-water rescue — the rescue of a paddler performed "out at sea", necessary because the person in trouble is too far from an easily-accessible shore.

Paddle — a simple but rather innovative tool that allows one to translate human power into elaborate boat movements. Kayakers, of course, use a double-bladed paddle, so unlike a one-bladed paddle (such as that used with a canoe), one can paddle on either side of the kayak without the need to move the paddle from one side of the boat to the other.

Paddle float — a small, inflatable float bag that fits over and attaches to the blade of a paddle. When it's is inflated and attached, and the other end of the paddle is attached to a kayak at a right angle (such as to cargo lines behind the seat or cockpit), the paddle can be used as an outrigger to stabilize the boat for re-entry during **self-rescue**. If you are alone in open water and do not know how to roll, this is your next best self-rescue option assuming the water is calm, your paddle can be attached to the kayak as needed, and you are familiar with this rescue technique.

There are also **paddle blocks** which do the same thing but do not require inflation; they are foam blocks that simply strap on to the paddle's blade.

The technique for using either of these, however, is beyond the scope of recreational kayaking and this book.

Paddle signals — signals made using your paddle to communicate to others on the trip. These are better than shouting and more communicative than a whistle. Make sure everyone in the group knows the signals being used before heading out. If a paddle is not available use your arms. Signals common in North America are given in the "GENERAL KAYAKING RECOMMENDATIONS" section.

Paddling pants — waterproof pants with rubber or neoprene gaskets around the waist and ankles. (See also **spray top**.)

PFD — personal floatation device. For kayakers, this will be a USCG-approved, Type III (or better, if needed) life jacket. The three PFD types are defined in the "LIFE JACKET / PFD" section.

Pillar — in the bow or stern of a sit-inside kayak without a bulkhead, this is a vertical piece that's typically 4"-thick, waterproof, foam rubber held in place in some simple way. The primary purpose of a pillar is to provide structural support, especially if the kayak should it become pinned against an obstacle and the current attempts to collapse it. If your kayak came with a pillar never use the boat without it.

Foam pillars also provide a little bit of floatation. If there are pillars at each end, you are not in the kayak, and it fills with water — it may just barely float. So foam pillars are the bare minimum of **floatation** required. But **float bags** are much better and **bulkheads** are best because both fill the end of the kayak displacing a whole lot more water.

Pillow — on a river, the raised, upstream "hump" on the surface of the water caused by a rock, boulder, or similar obstacle that is just above, at, or just below the surface. The exact position and size of the obstacle is often hard to tell from the size of the pillow as that varies with the shape of the obstacle, how deep it resides, and the speed of the current.

Point boat — a.k.a. lead boat — the boat at the front of the group. (See also **sweep boats**.)

Polyethylene — the type of plastic used in the **rotomolding** process and commonly used for recreational, whitewater, and inexpensive sea kayaks.

Portage — to carry a boat over land, going around a dam or obstruction blocking a river or from one paddleable body of water to another.

Power face — the front face of a paddle's blade. It catches the water when paddling forward. (See also **back face**.)

Power stroke — a paddle stroke the propels the kayak forward the most and turns it the least. To make this stroke, spread your hands farther apart than normal, place the paddle very close to the kayak in an almost vertical position, and pull parallel to the centerline of the boat.

Pry stroke — a stroke made by placing the paddle very close to the boat then pushing away from it.

When done at the stern, the **stern pry stroke** is a simple and effective way to the turn the kayak and best used when moving. To do this, turn the paddle's blade vertical and place it in the water behind you near the boat. Then push out, away from the kayak. Combined with a **stern draw stroke**, you're using the paddle as a rudder — called a **stern rudder stroke**.

There's also a **bow pry stroke** but it's not as effective (except at the beginning of a **sweep stroke**).

Put-in — the starting **access point** of a paddle trip — where boats are put in the water. (See also **take-out**.)

Quartering sea — waves or swells coming from the front or rear quarter. Typically the term is used to describe a front quartering sea — one that's roughly 45 degrees off the bow. (See also **following sea** and **head sea**.)

Quartering wind — a **crosswind** coming from the front or rear quarter. (See also **headwind** and **tailwind**.)

Rapids — a section of river with a relatively steep gradient and sometimes narrower channel causing an increase in water velocity and/or a section with water that bounces between numerous rocks causing an increase in turbulence and creating whitewater.

Read the river — while **boat scouting**, the act of continually looking ahead on the river to see what the water and current is doing, especially at obstacles and around turns.

Rear quarter — while traveling in a boat, the quarter-circle of horizontal area from that directly (90 degrees) at the side to directly behind the boat. There's a left rear quarter and a right rear quarter. (See also **front quarter**, **quartering sea**, and **quartering wind**.)

Recreational kayak — a class of "general purpose" kayaks designed for the casual paddler interested in recreational activities on **recreational kayak water**. Compared to **whitewater** and **sea kayaks**, they're more stable, have a larger **cockpit**, and are easier to use. Many of their properties are in between a whitewater and a sea kayak:

- They are faster, more efficient, and **track** better but turn poorer than a whitewater kayak.
- They turn easier but are slower, less efficient, and track poorer than a sea kayak.

Recreational kayaks are often used for photography, wildlife observation, and fishing where maximum stability is of primary importance as the paddler focuses on other things. They are typically made from **rotomolded polyethylene** which is the least expensive and heaviest yet most durable kayak material.

Recreational kayak water — flatwater, close to shore on very calm larger bodies of water, and relatively easy rivers through **Class II**. (See **classification of rivers**.)

Recreational kayaking — Using a **recreational kayak** while paddling **recreational kayak water**.

Reverse sweep stroke — a **sweep stroke** done in reverse which both turns the kayak and backs it up.

Riffle — a.k.a. swift — a region of tiny waves, small ripples, or light turbulence on a river, typically over a shallow area that's a "field" of smaller-sized rocks.

Rip cord — a.k.a. release loop — the cord or strap at the front of a **spray skirt** used to remove it quickly. When attaching the spray skirt to a kayak be sure the rip cord is hanging out and not tucked in!

Rip rap — a.k.a. riprap or rip-rap — large chunks of rock or concrete used to line a shore, river bank, bridge abutment, piling, or other structure to prevent scour and erosion caused by the water.

Rise — a term used in this book to describe the often abrupt change in the **keel** at the ends of a kayak, mostly above the **waterline**, where the **rocker** ends and the keel line goes up to meet the kayak's **deck** or **top-side**. Most whitewater kayaks have no definite rise as their keel is one continuous arc (rocker). The keel for recreational and sea kayaks, on the other hand, usually has a only small amount of rocker then a somewhat abrupt rise at the ends. See **Drawing B** in the "Kayak Keel" section.

River classification — see **classification of rivers**.

River dynamics — the behavior of the moving water of a river.

River left — the left side of the river when facing **downstream**.

River right — the right side of the river when facing **downstream**.

River surfing — the same as ocean surfing but done on a river in a large **standing wave**, facing upstream, and not actually moving forwards or backwards relative to the shore.

Rocker — the amount of curve in the majority of the keel below the waterline of the boat. The more rocker the more easily a boat will turn and the poorer it will **track**. Whitewater kayaks have a lot of rocker; sea kayaks have very little. The rocker on recreational kayaks is somewhere in between. See **Drawing B** in the "Kayak Keel" section for one example.

Roll — once called an "Eskimo" roll as it was created by the originators of the kayak — to completely roll a kayak over and back up while staying in the kayak. Knowing how to roll is an essential **self-rescue** technique for whitewater and sea kayakers. It's something that most recreational kayakers will likely never do, in part because it would be difficult to impossible to do with most recreational kayaks.

Rotomolding — short for rotational molding, the process where the mold gets rotated during the **polyethylene** cooking process. Manufacturers use rotomolding because it allows them to make long, hollow shapes such as kayaks.

Rudder — a movable blade mounted at the stern of a kayak (or any boat). Although it can be used as a steering device, it's primarily used to maintain a course when traveling in wind, waves, and/or current. Typically controlled by foot pedals, the rudder swivels from left to right. It's raised and lowered via lines from the cockpit. When not in use the rudder rides outside the water, often on top of the stern of the deck. (This should not be confused with the **stern rudder stroke**.)

When a rudder is in use correcting a kayak's direction it increases the drag slightly, so it takes a little more effort to go the same distance. When not in use a rudder increases the kayak's exposure to wind at the stern, further trying to turn the boat into the wind.

Sand bar — see **bar** and also **shoal**.

Scooch — a.k.a. scoot or scootch — at least as used in this book, to slide a kayak a short distance while remaining seated in it by jerking one's hips or whole body, such as to scooch over a low log on which one is stuck.

Sculling — a stroke where the paddle is moved back and forth a short distance in a continuous looping motion, somewhat figure-8-like, and while doing so changing the angle of the blade slightly with each pass, causing the boat to move in the direction perpendicular to that motion, such as forward or sideways. Sculling can also be used as a bracing stroke when at rest to regain or maintain one's balance. The motion is very similar to spreading frosting on a cake or peanut butter on bread. More details follow.

A boat can be moved *forward* by sculling at its stern. With some boats this is done via a single mounted oar. To scull in a kayak, the paddle is held at the side parallel to it with one blade placed vertically in the water near the stern. As the paddle is sculled back and forth a short distance, the angle of the blade is changed slightly, moving the kayak forward a little with each stroke. This is not a very effective way to move forward but it's fun while relaxed on a lazy section of river. You will move forward slowly by keeping your paddle in more or less the same place and do not have to take it out of the water.

A kayak can be moved *sideways* by sculling back and forth on the side. It's called a **sculling draw stroke** and done with the paddle shaft at a steep, almost vertical angle. As the paddle is sculled back and forth a short distance, the angle of the blade is changed slightly, moving the kayak sideways a little with each stroke. The kayak is pulled towards the paddle's position. It's more effective than a **sideways draw stroke** to move a boat directly sideways; although it's slower it provides more control and stability. Though you are not likely to need this stroke very often it can be handy when needing to carefully move sideways such as up to a landing that's parallel to the shore.

There's also a **sculling pry stroke** where the kayak is pushed away from the paddle's position, but it's much less effective than a sculling draw and somewhat hazardous to maintaining the stability of the boat.

You can also scull on the side of the kayak while sitting in place with the paddle shaft at shallow angle. Called a **sculling brace stroke** it's a way to *brace* yourself as well as regain and/or maintain your balance. The convenience of this stroke is that your paddle never comes out of the water so it's continually providing support, as might be needed with a strong **crosswind** or following a **high** or **low brace**.

Scupper holes — a.k.a. scuppers — in a sit-on-top kayak, self-bailing holes in the depressions in the **top-side** through which water drains out. Note that water can travel up these holes but normally does not.

Sea kayak — a sit-inside kayak used for paddling on the open waters of lakes, bays, and oceans. These are long, fast, very efficient, and track very well, yet are quite tippy and hard to turn. Sometimes they are incorrectly called a **touring kayak**. Of the modern kayaks these most resemble the original kayaks.

Sea sock — a large, waterproof bag in which one sits in a sit-inside kayak. It's fastened securely around the cockpit coaming under a spray skirt. It is used especially with "skin-on-frame" kayaks as their type of construction makes bulkheads impractical. It is also used in a standard sit-inside kayak in addition to bulkheads or float bags as an extra "line of defense" to prevent water from filling up the kayak. (Note, however, that a sea sock should never be used in place of proper **floatation**.) Although appreciated by serious sea and touring kayakers this is something the average recreational kayaker should not ever need.

Self-rescue — the act of rescuing oneself, such as rolling or climbing from the water back into or onto one's boat without the help of others. These techniques are beyond the scope of recreational kayaking and this book but are certainly covered in any sea kayaking class.

Shaft — the cylindrical middle part of a double-bladed paddle between the blades onto which the paddler grabs.

Shoal — an area of very shallow water especially as a navigational hazard. It may also be a rocky area, sandbank, **sand bar,** or **gravel bar**, and especially a region that is exposed above the surface of the water during low water level. (See also **bar**.)

Shock cord — a.k.a. stretch cord or bungee cord — elastic cord made from multiple strands of rubber wrapped with cotton or polypropylene. It is often used as cargo line on the deck or top-side of a kayak. It's available in bulk and in various lengths with hooks on each end. (This is the type of cord that's used when bungee jumping. It's not the same as **bungee strap**.)

Shuttle plan — the exact plan of how **shuttling** will occur.

Shuttling — the act of moving people, equipment, and vehicles before and after a paddle trip between the **put-in** and **take-out** points.

Sideways draw stroke — see **draw stroke**.

Sit-inside kayak — a traditional kayak with a **deck** enclosing the **hull**. One gets into it via an opening in the deck called a **cockpit**. Note however that the cockpit in some **recreational kayaks** is so large the boat can hardly be called "enclosed".

Sit-on-top kayak — a.k.a. sit-upon, open-top, and wash-deck kayak — a kayak without an enclosing **deck** — one sits "on top" of it within a molded cavity in the **top-side** for one's seat, legs, and feet. There are usually other cavities to accommodate gear.

Skeg — a fin-like blade that protrudes from the bottom of a kayak near the stern that acts like a fixed **rudder** to help **track** and maintain directional stability especially when traveling in wind, waves, and/or current. As it's fixed in place (does not swivel) it's not as effective as a rudder. But a skeg **does** tilt up and down — its depth is controlled via a line or lever near the cockpit. A skeg tucks up into a pocket (called the skeg box) in the hull so it's nicely out of way when not in use.

Spray skirt — a.k.a. spray deck or spray cover — for a sit-inside kayak, a specialized piece of gear made from waterproof fabric that seals around the paddler's chest or waist and the cockpit coaming of the boat thereby preventing water from entering the cockpit.

Spray top — a.k.a. spray jacket or paddling jacket — a waterproof jacket or anorak with rubber or neoprene gaskets around the waist, wrists, and neck. The better ones have a zipper at the neck to allow ventilation when desired. (See also **paddling pants**.)

Standing wave — a fixed wave of flowing water in a river such as that immediately downstream from an obstacle or caused by the topography of the river bottom. These can be quite small to being large enough to **river surf**.

Stern — the rear of a boat. (See also **bow**.)

Stern draw stroke — see **draw stroke**.

Stern float — in a sit-inside kayak, some form of floatation in the rear of the boat. The ideal stern float completely fills that end of the kayak. (See also **bow float** and **float bag**.)

Stern pry stroke — see **pry stroke**.

Stern rudder stroke — using **stern draw** and **stern pry strokes** to steer a kayak. This is very handy when guiding yourself down a river, running with **following seas**, surfing the front of a wave, and **river surfing**. The further back you place the paddle the more influence you have on the turn. You can control your direction to a minor extent when making this stroke by holding the paddle in place and slightly rotating the shaft (called **feathering**) one way or the other.

Strainer — a obstacle or set of obstacles in a river that lets water pass through but not boats or people. A collection of fallen trees and log jams are great examples. A tight grouping of boulders, patches of willows and other larger shrubbery growing in the river, even a wire fence in the water can be a strainer. These are made worse because they can collect driftwood, **tree-fall**, and other debris. They can be very dangerous and should be avoided if at all possible.

Sunstroke — see **heat stroke.**

Swamp — to fill a sit-inside kayak with water. A swamped boat is one that's completely filled with water.

Sweep boats — the TWO boats at the rear of the group. (See also **point boat.**)

Sweep stroke — a wide-arcing stroke in the form a large letter "C" used to turn a kayak.

Sweeper — overhanging obstacles above moving water, typically low-hanging branches over a river, that can "sweep" one from his/her boat or tip it over.

Swimmer — a kayaker in trouble in the water out of his/her kayak.

Tailwind — wind coming from directly behind you in line with your direction of travel. (See also **crosswind, headwind,** and **quartering wind.**)

Take-out — a.k.a. pull-out point — the end **access point** of a paddle trip where boats are taken out of the water. (See also **put-in**.)

Tandem kayak — a two-person (a.k.a. double or K-2) kayak. These are fun but to use effectively they require a fair amount of additional skills and paddling instruction compared to a single-person kayak (K-1).

Technical — an aspect of an activity or an area of practice of that activity requiring significant skill, effort, ability, technique, and/or maneuvering. For river paddlers two examples are: a *technical* section of a river, and a Class III river is much more *technical* than a Class I.

Thigh braces — a.k.a. knee braces, knee hooks, or thigh hooks — in a sit-inside kayak, these are parts added to or molded into the area of the cockpit opening near where one's thighs or knees touch the edge of that opening. (See **Photo 1** in the "Kayak Thigh Braces" section for one example.) Or they can be simply a well-designed cockpit opening that crosses over one's thighs in a comfortable way. Used together with **foot rests**, one can "lock" one's legs in place under these braces gaining great control of the kayak when leaning, **edging**, or maintaining one's balance. Thigh braces are essential for whitewater and sea kayakers and imperative to do any type of a **roll**. They are very helpful for recreational paddlers, as well.

Throat — On a paddle where the blade tapers to meet the shaft.

Throw bag — a.k.a. throw rope — a rope attached to and coiled in a nylon bag with other end free. While holding the free end, the bag is easily thrown to (or upstream of) a kayaker in trouble. The rope uncoils from the bag while it's in flight. (It's also recommended to carry a rescue knife in case the rope ever needs to be quickly cut for some reason.)

Tidal current — a current caused by the rise and fall of tides in channels connected to large bodies of water with tides. River currents are due to Earth's gravity; tides are due to the gravity of our moon and sun. (See also **current**.)

Strong tidal currents can be quite hazardous. If you will be paddling in any tidal zone (area where there are tides), be sure to fully understand the tides in that area before venturing out. See the *www.saltwatertides.com* Web site for more information.

Top-side — on a sit-on-top kayak, the top half of the boat spanning its length and width (going across the **gunwales**) enclosing the **hull**. Unlike the arched **deck** of a sit-inside kayak, the top-side is somewhat sunken in with molded cavities for the paddler and some gear.

Top-side rigging — lines, typically elastic shock cord, attached to the top-side of a sit-on-top kayak used to secure cargo. These lines should not be used to carry the kayak. (See also **deck rigging**.)

Touring — going on an extended kayak trip from a few days to several weeks in length, camping along the way, and typically using a **touring kayak**. Touring can be done with many types of kayaks — sea kayaks are good but **touring kayaks** are the most suitable.

Touring kayak — similar to a **sea kayak** but more stable, more comfortable, slightly wider and shorter, and carries more cargo. It may sometimes be called an *expedition kayak*.

Tow line — a quick-release line attached from a rescuer (usually at the waist) in a kayak to another kayak or **swimmer**.

Track — the ability for a kayak to go straight. Sea kayaks track incredibly well while **whitewater kayaks**, by design, do not track well at all. **Recreational kayaks** are somewhere in between. The better a kayak tracks the harder it is to turn, and visa versa.

Tree-fall — trees that have fallen into the river. They may or may not be attached to the shore. They can easily become **strainers** especially if they break free and combine together. If there are enough of them together they can become an **obstruction**. (If not in the water yet, falling and fallen trees may be **sweepers**.)

Be prepared for tree-fall on any river that flows through forested land, even if that land is quite a ways upstream. River sections popular with paddlers should have at least a path cut through any tree-fall by outfitters, liveries, guide services, local paddling groups, and/or other river-friendly organizations or individuals. Know that new tree-fall can appear at anytime but especially after a heavy rain or spring-floods. Those will also carry tree-fall downstream where it might get caught in deep holes, snagged against other tree-fall, or deposited on shoals, at the head of islands, and along the banks.

Trip plan — for any paddle trip, when and where to meet ahead of time, the exact put-in and take-out points, start and end times, specific paddle route, scheduled stops along the way, etc. Make sure everyone going knows the trip plan. At least one responsible person not on the trip needs to be aware of the plan and the names of everyone on the trip.

Upstream — on a river, the direction from which the water is flowing towards you. (See also **downstream**.)

Upwind — the direction the wind is from; to go into or against the wind. (See also **downwind**.)

Waterline — the line of intersection along which the surface of the water contacts a boat's **hull**, especially when it's floating with its normal amount of weight.

Waterline length — the length of a boat at its waterline, usually several inches less than the overall length on a typical kayak.

Weathercock — a.k.a. weather helm — the tendency of a boat to turn into the wind, that is, **upwind**. The opposite of **leecock**. Often a **crosswind** can more easily push the stern of a kayak than the bow, so that type wind will try to turn the boat into the wind. A **skeg**, or better yet a **rudder**, can help lessen this effect. Otherwise, with any degree of crosswind, you'll need to paddle much more on one side of the kayak than the other. **Edging** your kayak to the **windward** side should lessen weathercocking a little, which is yet another time when **thigh braces** will help.

Wet exit — leaving a kayak while it's upside down (or almost) and going into the water, usually unintentionally.

Wet suit — a very close-fitting suit of neoprene rubber designed to prevent or greatly slow down heat loss when you are submerged in cold water. It operates by trapping a thin layer of water next to your skin, keeping you warm.

Wet suits are available in a variety of thicknesses and styles. Thinner wet suits do not keep you as warm but allow more freedom of movement. "Shortie" wet suits cover you the least but are still much more effective at keeping a wet kayaker warm than any type of clothing.

A wet suit is recommended if the water temperature is 55 degrees Fahrenheit or less, and imperative if it's below 50 degrees.

The only thing more effective than a wet suit to keep a person warm and dry in cold and wet conditions is a *dry suit* (a close-fitting, air-insulated, waterproof suit with gaskets that seal around one's neck, wrists. and ankles), the use of which is out of the realm of recreational kayaking.

Whitewater — frothy water formed in a **rapid** where there is so much turbulence that air is trapped in the water. It forms a very bubbly and unstable current of water appearing white.

Whitewater kayak — a kayak used for paddling a fast-moving body of water, typically a **whitewater** river. (See **classification of rivers**.) These are very short, can turn extremely easily and fast, but are not very efficient and do not track well at all, by design. These are a relatively recent development and are perhaps the most removed from the design of the original kayak.

Width (kayak) — a.k.a. **beam** — the width of a kayak at its widest point.

Windward side — the side of an object facing the wind. (See also **lee side**.)

Yak — Among paddlers an abbreviation sometimes used for kayak. (Also, a shaggy-haired domesticated wild ox found in Tibet that would be very difficult to ride upon in the water. ☺)

> **RECOMMENDATION**: Go forth and have a great time on the water!!

A Place for Your Notes....

Made in the USA
Lexington, KY
19 May 2018